The Illustrated

Wineries
of
the Napa
Valley

The Illustrated Guide to

Wineries of the Napa Valley

Selected Day-Trips to Local Gems
written and illustrated by
Richard Golueke

Foreword by Jac Cole,
Napa Valley Consulting Winemaker

To my dad

The Illustrated Guide to Wineries of the Napa Valley
© 2012 Richard Golueke

ISBN: 978-0-9893954-0-3
Catalog in Publication on record with the Library of Congress
03.02

Cover Credits:
Richard Golueke

"I cook with wine. Sometimes I even add it to the food."
— W. C. Fields

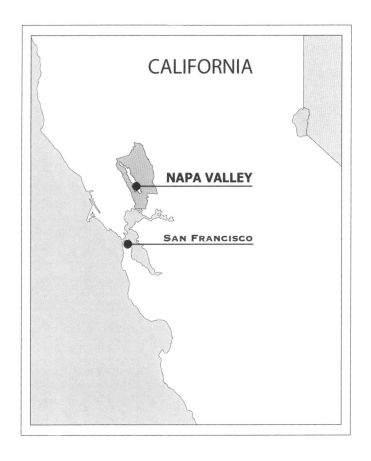

CONTENTS

Table of Contents

Villa Miravalle, Spring Mountain Vineyard

FOREWORD

With hundreds of world-class wineries and dozens of the most highly regarded restaurants in the country, Napa Valley is one of the top wine and food destinations in the world. But with the myriad possibilities and limitations of time and distance, how does one decide where to go and what to experience? One excellent answer is in your hands right now, Richard Golueke's *The Illustrated Guide to Wineries of the Napa Valley*.

Richard and I have been friends for more years than either of us would care to admit, and we've traveled together often, from the hills of California's Gold Country to the golden hills of Rome. Richard has always had a keen eye for the unique, off-the-beaten path experience.

As a Bay Area native, Richard has been visiting the Napa Valley for decades and has experienced for himself the common pitfall of trying to do too much in too little time. This book is his thoughtful approach to help travelers choose a memorable Napa Valley itinerary, one that is both relaxed and fulfilling. Richard's guide breaks Napa Valley into delicious, bite-sized pieces that will yield great memories and minimize frustration.

So, read along and build your Napa Valley adventure from the rich and varied possibilities. Whether you are looking for the best wines or stunning vistas, I hope you enjoy this beautiful place I'm blessed to call home.

Jac Cole,
Napa Valley
Consulting Winemaker

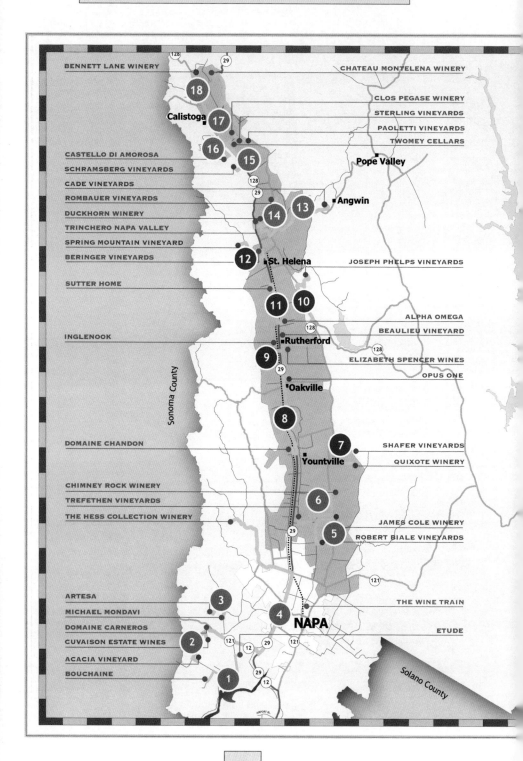

BENNETT LANE WINERY
CHATEAU MONTELENA WINERY
CLOS PEGASE WINERY
STERLING VINEYARDS
PAOLETTI VINEYARDS
TWOMEY CELLARS
Calistoga
Pope Valley
CASTELLO DI AMOROSA
SCHRAMSBERG VINEYARDS
CADE VINEYARDS
ROMBAUER VINEYARDS
DUCKHORN WINERY
TRINCHERO NAPA VALLEY
SPRING MOUNTAIN VINEYARD
BERINGER VINEYARDS
Angwin
SUTTER HOME
St. Helena
JOSEPH PHELPS VINEYARDS
ALPHA OMEGA
BEAULIEU VINEYARD
INGLENOOK
Rutherford
ELIZABETH SPENCER WINES
OPUS ONE
Oakville
Sonoma County
DOMAINE CHANDON
SHAFER VINEYARDS
QUIXOTE WINERY
Yountville
CHIMNEY ROCK WINERY
TREFETHEN VINEYARDS
THE HESS COLLECTION WINERY
JAMES COLE WINERY
ROBERT BIALE VINEYARDS
ARTESA
THE WINE TRAIN
MICHAEL MONDAVI
NAPA
DOMAINE CARNEROS
ETUDE
CUVAISON ESTATE WINES
ACACIA VINEYARD
BOUCHAINE
Solano County

XCURSION NUMBER
XX
NO APPOINTMENT

BY APPOINTMENT

Yolo County

WELCOME TO THE NAPA VALLEY:

Eighteen Day-Trips to Thirty-Six Wineries

From Etude to
Bennett Lane Winery

KEY:	Napa Wineries	
Green:	NO APPOINTMENT REQUIRED	
Red:	APPOINTMENT REQUIRED	
TRIP ROUTES:		
	LOWER VALLEY ▬▬ x ▬▬	
	MID VALLEY ▬ x ▬	
	UPPER VALLEY ▬ x ▬	

INTRODUCTION

Getting More Out of Your Winery Visits

By some accounts about 4.5 million tourists and wine enthusiasts visit over 300 wineries in the Napa Valley every year. Many visitors are overly ambitious and typically try to see and do too much in too little time. A common problem for many people is not knowing what wineries to visit or even where to start.

My solution to minimize this frustration is to provide visitors with a simple guidebook that outlines specific places, times and tours. I drill down on the broad and often overwhelming number of general guidebook recommendations and focus on 18 specific, pre-planned, afternoon wine-tasting trips to 36 wineries and their respective tasting rooms. I augment tasting-room descriptions, tour schedules and winery histories with maps, my own hand-drawn illustrations and suggestions for nearby dining.

So the premise of this book is to arrange unique and interesting wineries and their tasting rooms into a series of pre-planned, no-hassle excursions that in effect take you by the hand and show you what to see. The overall mission is to make Napa Valley wineries more approachable and more inviting for more visitors. The result is a more relaxed and enjoyable wine-tasting experience.

For locals and visitors beginning their tasting from within the Napa Valley, this book can be used as a general guide to nearby wineries. For those who would like to visit more wineries than are covered in a particular afternoon's excursion or for those planning a full day of tasting, simply add the next pre-planned trip or trips in the book to your itinerary. If you're interested in tours, just make sure the wineries' tour schedules correspond with your planned arrivals.

I try to give you an idea of what to expect at each stop: whether you need to make an appointment, hours of operation, tour info, phone numbers or website info, a little background information about each winery and how much it might cost.

Tasting and tour price ranges are for the basic tastings and tours. Check winery websites for additional options and prices. Wineries *frequently* change how they schedule and what they charge for tastings and tours, so it is wise to check before visiting. You can use this guide to see how expensive one winery might be relative to another but other details will likely change over time. For wineries requiring reservations, many only require an hour or so of advance notification. Others prefer 24 hours or more. Call ahead or check their websites for reservation preferences.

I also include some basic restaurant recommendations. Again, I have paired them with the wineries you may be visiting. Obviously if you're visiting, say, the Upper Napa Valley, it would be quite easy to swing by a recommended restaurant in the Lower Valley as long as it's on your way.

A word about how the book is organized. It takes roughly 45 minutes to drive from one end of the valley to the other. I've divided it into a Lower, Mid and Upper Napa Valley so that driving time should be no more than 15 minutes from one winery to another, top to bottom, within each division. Not only does this minimize travel time but it helps concentrate your efforts to what otherwise might be an overwhelming number of winery choices. Trips are numbered only for the purpose of identification. Feel free to begin your tour in the Upper Valley or Mid Valley if you prefer. It is perfectly fine to do your excursions in reverse numerical order or from somewhere in-between if you wish.

Finally, we make no judgment regarding the wines. It is the overall experience of visiting a winery, in which the quality of the wine is but one of many factors, that is the subject of this book. A winery that produces indifferent wine may be worth a visit for any number of other reasons. The grounds, the staff, the cost, the educational aspects and the entertainment value all play an important part. Similarly, a winery with a reputation of producing great wine may be worth a visit for that alone.

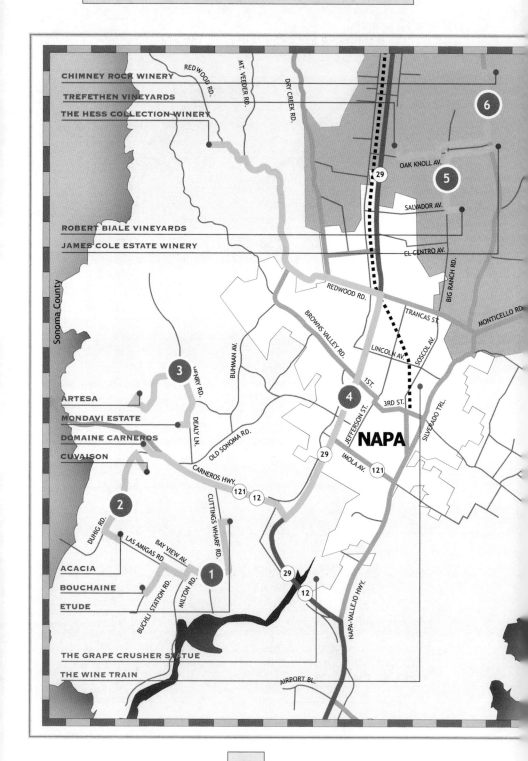

XCURSION NUMBER

XX

NO APPOINTMENT

BY APPOINTMENT

121

LOWER NAPA VALLEY:

Six Day-Trips to Twelve Lower Valley Wineries

From Etude to
Chimney Rock Winery

KEY:	Winery Guide	
Green: NO APPOINTMENT		**Red: BY APPOINTMENT**
COST PER PERSON		
Nominal.......(0 - $14)..........**$**		
Moderate.....($15 - $29).....**$$**		
Elevated.......($30 - $44).....**$$$**		
Spendy.........($45 PLUS).....**$$$$**		

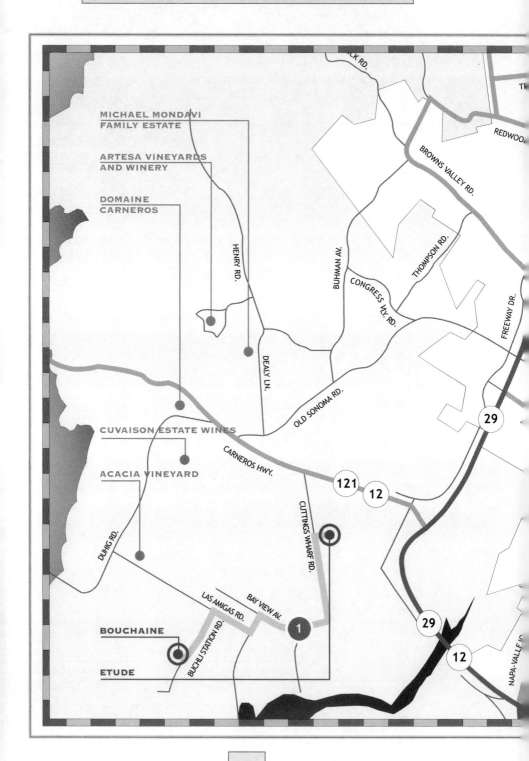

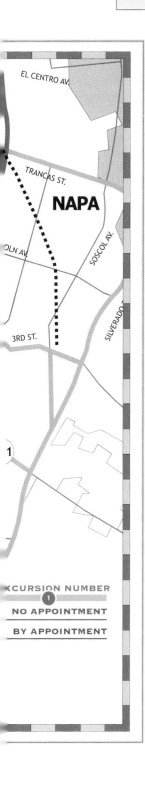

1

ETUDE TO BOUCHAINE

Off the Beaten Path:

Begin your exploration of Napa Valley wineries in the Carneros, the southern-most region of the Napa Valley. Known for its exceptional Pinot Noirs and Chardonnays, it is often overlooked by first-time visitors.

Etude: The tasting room for Etude Wines is very modern with high ceilings and a contemporary decor. Drop-ins are welcome throughout the day and a five-wine Premium tasting is offered. In addition to the Premium tasting, a five-wine Reserve tasting is available Friday through Sunday. Food and wine pairings are also offered, at 10 am, 1 pm and 3 pm by appointment. While Etude produces a limited quantity of several varietals, it specializes in Pinot Noir and Cabernet Sauvignon. Enjoy a leisurely tasting on the back patio under umbrellaed tables.

Bouchaine: A ten minute drive takes you to Bouchaine. No appointment is necessary for six or fewer visitors but is required for larger groups. There are currently no winery or vineyard tours offered. A self-guided 1.2 mile vineyard walk is available at no charge. Picnics are reserved for club members only. Two tiers of tastings are available: the Bacchus and the Estate. You may have your tastings either inside at the bar or, for an additional charge, outside on the patio. The additional charge for tasting on the patio includes a cheese and olive plate. Purchase two bottles and your *inside* tasting fee for one person is waived. Purchase three bottles and your *patio* tasting fee for one person is waived.

17

Etude Wines

Etude is a term in classical music which refers to a composition with a technical focus that allows the musician to hone and improve on a specific technique. This is the metaphor that Etude utilizes in its winemaking. According to founder and "winegrower", Tony Soter, Pinot Noir is the most challenging and unforgiving of grapes but when the technique is mastered, produces a glorious result.

Since its inception in 1982, Etude has been renowned for its world-class Pinot Noir and Cabernet Sauvignon. Etude produces limited quantities of Pinot Gris, Pinot Blanc and Merlot which are also well regarded.

Although Tony Soter now focuses exclusively on his Oregon winery, Soter Vineyards, his influence on Etude continues to this day. As a consultant to many wineries in the Napa Valley, he purchased grapes by the acre rather than by the ton which encouraged growers to lower yields which, in turn, produced better quality grapes. His approach was to get as much as possible from the grapes in the vineyard and to minimize intrusion by the winemaker. At Etude, superior wines are as a result, grown, not made.

ETUDE WINES	
WEBSITE:	www.etudewines.com
TASTING:	**$$**/5 tastes Premium (daily), **$$**/5 tastes Reserve (F - Sun)
APPOINTMENT:	Required for Wine & Food Pairing and groups of 6 or more
ADDRESS:	1250 Cuttings Wharf Rd.,
	Napa, CA 94559
PHONE:	1+(877) 586-9361 or (707) 257-5300
HOURS:	Daily, 10 am - 4:30 pm
TOURS:	No tour. **$$$**/5 tastes Wine & Food Pairing, 10 am, 1 & 3 pm (F - Sun)

Bouchaine

Bouchaine Vineyards, or simply Bouchaine, was purchased in 1927 by Italian immigrant Johnny Garetto. In 1981 it was acquired by Gerret and Tatiana Copeland of Wilmington, Delaware. Bouchaine is the oldest continually operated winery in Napa Valley's Carneros district. A massive renovation was completed in 1995 updating and refurbishing the facility to its current architecturally noteworthy state. The Copelands also purchased adjoining vineyard property giving the winery more than 100 acres of estate vineyards.

By 2000 Bouchaine had decided to make some changes in the style of wines they produced in a renewed effort to appeal to evolving consumer tastes. The Copelands hired Michael Richmond, founder of Acacia, to assume on-site winemaking and general management responsibilities. He and his team have since succeeded in bringing to market richer and more expressive wines that capture the elegance of Burgundy in the style of Carneros. Bouchaine produces about 25,000 cases, largely of Pinot Noir and Chardonnay. These grapes are especially suited to the fog and shallow clay loam soils of the region. Bouchaine also grows Pinot Gris and Pinot Meunier.

BOUCHAINE	
WEBSITE:	www.bouchaine.com
TASTING:	**$$**/5 tastes (**$$$** patio) Bacchus, **$$**/6 tastes (**$$$** patio) Estate
APPOINTMENT:	Required for groups of 6 or more
ADDRESS:	1075 Buchli Station Rd.,
	Napa, CA 94559
PHONE:	1+(800) 654-9463 or (707) 252-9065
HOURS:	Daily, 10:30 am - 4:30 pm (5:30 pm Mid-March to October)
TOURS:	Self-Guided Vineyard Walking Tour only

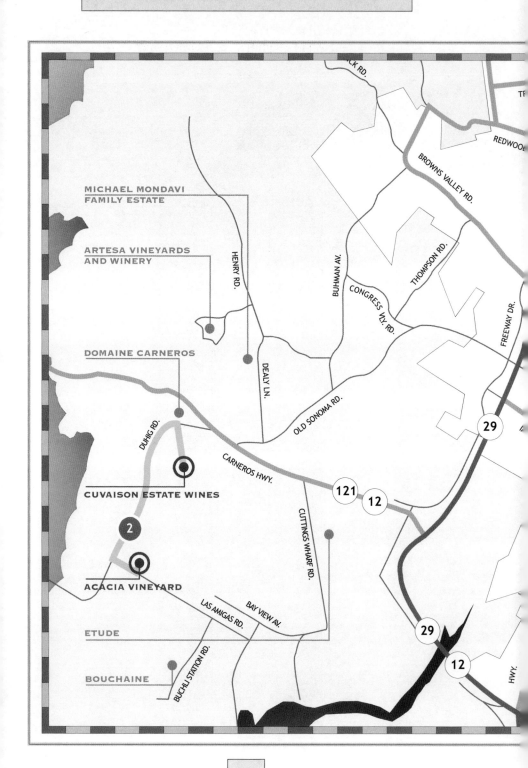

2

ACACIA TO CUVAISON

From Chardonnay to Pinot Noir:

Continue to Cuvaison and Acacia. Both are by appointment and neither offers a winery tour.

Acacia Vineyard: Acacia Vineyard's tasting room is quite intimate with a view of the interior workings of the winery through adjoining glass doors. Picnics are welcome and the setting affords vistas of the vineyards surrounding the winery. The winery itself is far removed from the tourist hustle and bustle found elsewhere in the Napa Valley and the rolling hills of the Carneros are beautiful. Pinot Noirs and Chardonnays are stand-outs here. Some popular wines are the Beckstoffer Pinot Noir, Winery Lake Pinot Noir, Lone Tree Pinot Noir, the Sangiacomo Chardonnay, the Marsh Chardonnay and the Late Harvest Chardonnay. The staff are exceptionally friendly and welcoming. Pours are moderately priced for six wines and don't forget that the fee can be applied towards a purchase of $25 or more.

Cuvaison Estate Wines: Cuvaison Estate Wines offers a 45-minute *Vineyard Walk and Tasting* at 9:30 am Friday through Monday mornings. Although no food is offered at the Carneros winery, you may bring your own picnic lunch to enjoy with your wine. Sit inside or take in the expansive views from the patio. Seated tastings of four wines are offered and a staff member will bring them to your table. Some popular wines from Cuvaison include its Chardonnays, Block 5 Pinot Noir and Cabernet Sauvignon from Mt. Veeder. Don't overlook the Petite Sirah and brandy-based Espiritu Port blend.

Acacia Vineyard

Acacia, which gets its name from the lone Acacia tree growing on its estate vineyard, was founded in 1979 by Michael Richmond, long-time friend Larry Brooks and one other financial partner. It was among the first California wineries to feature vineyard-designated wines and among the first dedicated to making Chardonnay and Pinot Noir in the Carneros region which was then, a promising but yet unproven area.

Acacia Winery was acquired by the Chalone Group in 1986 which at the time included Chalone Vineyard, Edna Valley Vineyard and Carmenet Vineyard. Michael Richmond and Larry Brooks remained for many years as Chalone Inc. employees: Michael in sales and management and Larry in winemaking.

Today Acacia produces about 100,000 cases of wine annually: mostly Pinot Noir and Chardonnay but also Sauvignon Blanc, Viogner and Syrah. The majority of its Pinot and Chardonnay come from two primary vineyards: the surrounding Acacia Vineyard and the nearby Winery Lake Vineyard.

ACACIA VINEYARD	
WEBSITE:	www.acaciavineyard.com
TASTING:	$$/5-6 tastes
APPOINTMENT:	Required 1 hr. in advance for weekday, 24 hrs. for weekend
ADDRESS:	2750 Las Amigas Road,
	Napa, CA 94559
PHONE:	1+(877) 226-1700 ext 2 or (707) 226-9991 ext 2
HOURS:	10 am - 4 pm (Mon - Sat), 12 pm - 4 pm (Sun)
TOURS:	$$$/5-6 tastes Tour & Tasting (Mon - Fri) @ 11 am

Cuvaison Estate Wines, Carneros

Cuvaison is a French word describing a step in the making of red wine where grape juice is kept in contact with the skins and seeds so that color, tannins and aroma are transferred to the juice.

Cuvaison Estate Wines has two winery and tasting room locations in the Napa Valley: one in Calistoga and one in Carneros. Its state-of-the-art solar powered winery in the Carneros district, completed in 2004, is arguably the premiere Chardonnay and Pinot Noir production facility in the Napa Valley.

The original Cuvaison winery was founded in 1969 in its Calistoga location by two Silicon Valley engineers: Thomas Cotrell and Thomas Parkhill. New York publisher Oakleigh Thorne purchased the winery and its 27-acre vineyard in 1974 and in 1979 the current owners, the Schmidheiny family of Switzerland, purchased Cuvaison along with 400 acres of vineyards in the Carneros district.

Although Cuvaison produces a variety of red and white wines, 65% of the 63,000 cases they produce annually are Chardonnay.

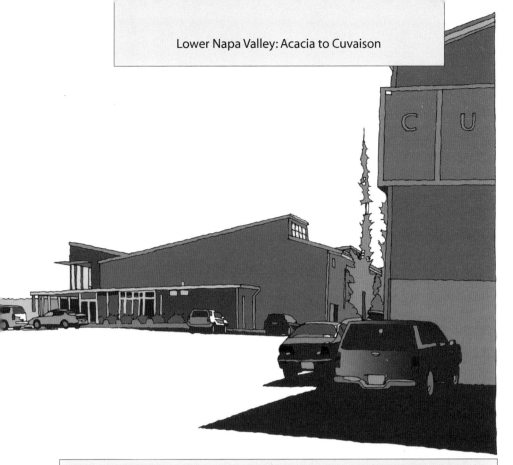

CUVAISON ESTATE WINES, CARNEROS	
WEBSITE:	www.cuvaison.com
TASTING:	$$/4 tastes Signature or Estate
APPOINTMENT:	Required 1 hr. in advance for weekday, 24 hrs. for weekend
ADDRESS:	1221 Duhig Rd.,
	Napa, CA 94559
PHONE:	(707) 942-2455
HOURS:	10 am - 4:30 pm (Th - Mon), 10 am - 4 pm (Tu - Wed)
TOURS:	$$$/ Vineyard Walk & Tasting, 9:30 am (Fri - Mon)

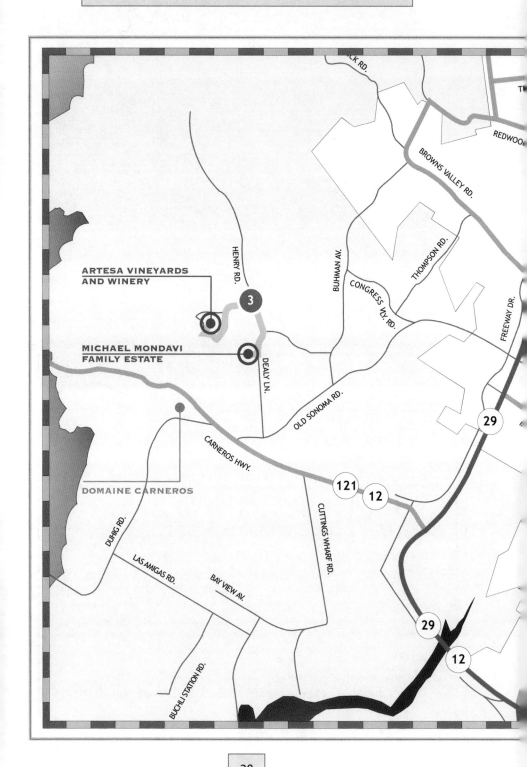

3

MONDAVI TO ARTESA

From Back Porch View to Hilltop Vista:

Since both Mondavi and Artesa are literally within sight of one another, your travel time between these wineries is minimal.

Michael Mondavi Family Estate: Set amidst the picturesque rolling hills of the Carneros district is Michael Mondavi Family Estate. No appointment is required although private tours do require advance arrangement. Try to be here around noon. You will be warmly greeted in the Taste Gallery and your wine-tasting experience will be relaxed and friendly. Take your wine out to the back terrace, find a couch and enjoy the view of the vineyard along with your picnic lunch if you wish. The wines are good and reasonably priced and the overall experience is satisfying.

Artesa Vineyards and Winery: If you're interested in a winery tour, the afternoon tour at Artesa Vineyards and Winery begins at 2 pm, lasts about 45 minutes and includes a tasting. If not, enjoy the views, location and architecture of the winery itself. The views here alone are worth the visit. The wines are also worthy so be sure to check out the tasting room. The ambiance can be a little high tech and not as intimate as some of the smaller wineries. Weekend crowds can be a bit off-putting. Tastings are reasonably priced. Feel free to wander throughout the first floor and outside onto the balcony with your glass and return to the bar for your next sample when ready. For something a little different try the Limited Release Albariño or Tempranillo Reserve.

Michael Mondavi Family Estate

After the sale of Robert Mondavi Winery to Constellation Brands in 2004, Robert's sons, Michael and Timothy, moved on to new challenges. Timothy and his sister Marcia founded Continuum Estate while Michael and his family established Folio Fine Wine Partners and Winemakers' Studio Winery.

Folio Winemakers' Studio Winery, now Michael Mondavi Family Estates, houses at least seven separate labels under one roof. Five labels are Mondavi produced: M by Michael Mondavi, Isabel Mondavi, Emblem, Spellbound and Medusa. The winemaker for these is Michael's son Rob who also oversees all wine production at the winery.

With the exception of M by Michael Mondavi, all of these wines may be sampled in the Taste Gallery. There is currently one tasting menu available. Offered for tasting are a Chardonnay, a Rosé, an Estate Pinot Noir and two Cabernet Sauvignons. Occasionally a reserve or single-vineyard wine, a wine of which 95% of the grapes are sourced from that specific vineyard, may be offered for tasting as well.

MICHAEL MONDAVI FAMILY ESTATE

WEBSITE:	www.michaelmondavifamilyestate.com
TASTING:	$$/5 tastes
APPOINTMENT:	Encouraged for groups of 7 or more
ADDRESS:	1285 Dealy Lane,
	Napa, CA 94559
PHONE:	(707) 256-2757
HOURS:	Daily, 11 am - 5 pm (last tasting at 4:30 pm)
TOURS:	For private tours & tastings call (707) 256-2757

Artesa Vineyards and Winery

Artesa is, hands down, one of the most beautiful wineries in the Napa Valley. The winery, which sits atop a hill and is covered with earth and native grasses, was designed by Barcelona architect Domingo Triay and built in the 1990's. In addition to the pools and water fountains, the views of the Carneros region and surrounding vineyards are breathtaking. Noted local artist, Gordon Huether, is the artist in residence and his sculptures and glass pieces adorn the Visitor Center.

Artesa, the Catalan word for "handcrafted", is part of the Codorníu Group, owned by the Raventós family of Spain. Codorníu is the original winemaking family name which harkens back to 1551.

Artesa's wines include Chardonnay and Pinot Noir from their Carneros vineyards and Merlot and Cabernet from vineyards in Napa and Sonoma Counties. Try the Limited Release Albariño and the Tempranillo Reserve. Albariño was originally a Portuguese white wine varietal and Tempranillo, a variety of black grape native to Spain, is often used in making Rioja wine.

ARTESA VINEYARDS AND WINERY	
WEBSITE:	*www.artesawinery.com*
TASTING:	***$$*/4 tastes Classic , *$$*/5 tastes Reserve, *$*/1 taste Sparkling*
APPOINTMENT:	*Required for groups of 8 or more*
ADDRESS:	*1345 Henry Road,*
	Napa, CA 94559
PHONE:	*1+(888) 679-9463 or (707) 224-1668*
HOURS:	*11 am - 5 pm (M - Th) , 10 am - 5 pm (F - Sun), (last pour 4:30 pm)*
TOURS:	***$$*/3 tastes daily tour & tasting (no appt.), 11 am & 2 pm*

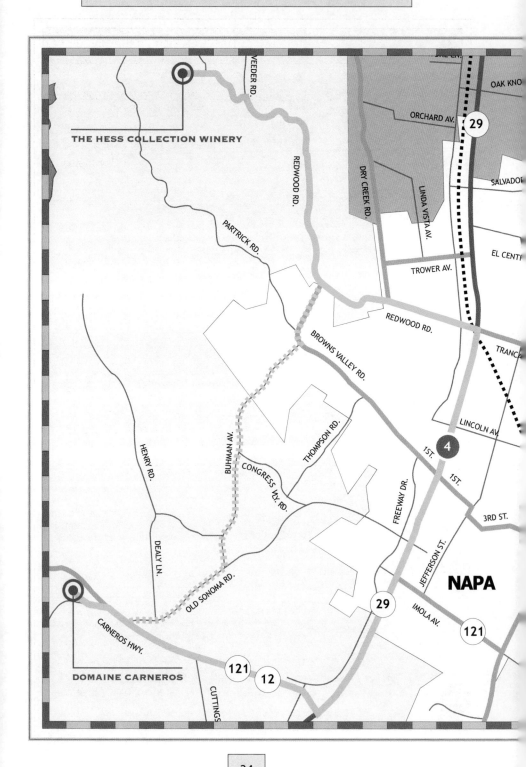

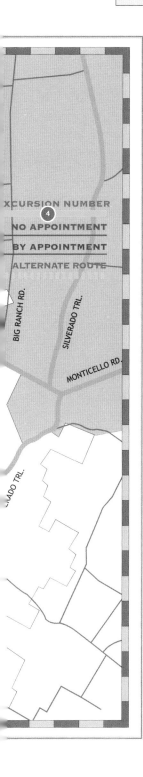

EXCURSION NUMBER
④

NO APPOINTMENT

BY APPOINTMENT

ALTERNATE ROUTE

BIG RANCH RD.

SILVERADO TRL.

MONTICELLO RD.

SILVERADO TRL.

④

CARNEROS TO HESS

Sparkling Wine and Sparkling Art:

Domaine Carneros: Start your tour at Taittenger's chateau-inspired Domaine Carneros winery. Try to be there no later than noon. Take some pictures, browse the gift shop, go sit out on the terrace, unwind and have a cheese plate with a glass of wine. The *Art of Sparkling Wine* tour is given at 11 am, 1 pm and 3 pm (also 4 pm, Saturdays, during peak season). Reservations, mainly for weekends or holidays, are recommended but not required. Large groups (10+) require reservations. The tour lasts about 90 minutes and includes some wine tasting both during and after the tour. Note, if your budget is a factor, consider skipping the Domaine tour, leave a little early and go on to Hess where the tours are free.

The Hess Collection Winery: Enjoy a drive a little off the beaten path to The Hess Collection where you will have the unique experience of taking in both a collection of fine contemporary art and a collection of fine wine. Tours are complimentary and are offered throughout the day from 10:30 am to 3:30 pm every hour on the half hour. Take the 45-minute tour and with whatever remains of the afternoon, visit the museum or go taste some wine in the tasting room. If you've already had the winery tour at Domaine Carneros, try concentrating on the three story museum which is free to the public and open until 5:15 pm. It has a wonderful collection of modern art. In the Spring, enjoy outdoor seating in the garden where you can order both wine and cheeses. Although not required, garden seating may be reserved on busy days by calling the winery.

Domaine Carneros

Domaine Carneros specializes in making sparkling wine and Pinot Noir. Their 18th century chateau-style winery was completed in 1989 as a joint project between the French champagne maker Taittinger and Kobrand Corporation. They purchased 138 acres of prime Carneros vineyards in the lower-most region of the Napa Valley. The climate and soil were ideal for Pinot Noir and Chardonnay, the prime components of their sparkling wine.

Domaine Carneros produces several sparkling wines: currently, *Brut Vintage*, *Brut Rosé* and *Le Rêve* ("the dream") *Blanc de Blancs*. A carriage house-like facility was opened behind the chateau in 2003 dedicated solely to making Pinot Noir. Today it offers various Pinot Noirs: *Avant-Garde, Domaine Carneros-Estate* and *The Famous Gate-Estate*.

Domaine Carneros prides itself on being an energy efficient and pesticide-free, "green", organic wine producer. In 2003 it installed the largest photovoltaic solar collection system of any winery in the world at the time.

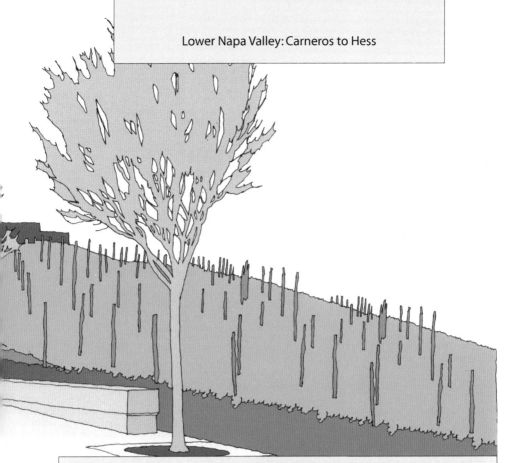

DOMAINE CARNEROS

WEBSITE:	www.domainecarneros.com
TASTING:	**$$**/3 tastes Sparkling, **$$**/4 tastes Chateau, **$$$**/4 tastes Grande
APPOINTMENT:	Suggested for weekends & holidays (required for 10 or more)
ADDRESS:	1240 Duhig Road,
	Napa, CA 94559
PHONE:	1+(800) 716-BRUT (2788)
HOURS:	Daily, 10 am - 6 pm (closed major holidays)
TOURS:	**$$$**/daily "Art of Sparkling Wine", 11 am, 1 pm and 3 pm

The Hess Collection

The Hess Collection was founded by Swiss entrepreneur Donald M. Hess in 1978 with his purchase of vineyards on Mt. Veeder. The winery is well known for its *Hess Collection Mount Veeder Estate* Cabernets and Chardonnays: complex and structured wines reflective of their mountain origins. It is also known for its *Hess Napa Valley* single-vineyard estate wines which are expressive of the unique qualities of soil, climate and topography imparted by special vineyards in Napa Valley.

Of perhaps equal importance is the Hess Collection of contemporary art which is available for public viewing free of charge. The winery houses one quarter of the art collection shown around the world. The museum is open daily between 10 am and 5 pm. Self-guided iPod® tours are also available at no charge.

Complimentary winery tours are available between 10:30 am and 3:30 pm daily. Check the website for other tour and tasting options. Special arrangements for larger groups may be made by calling the winery.

THE HESS COLLECTION	
WEBSITE:	www.hesscollection.com
TASTING:	**$$**/4 tastes
APPOINTMENT:	Required for groups of 9 or more
ADDRESS:	4411 Redwood Road,
	Napa, CA 94558
PHONE:	(707) 255-1144 or (707) 255-8584
HOURS:	Daily, 10 am - 5:30 pm
TOURS:	Free/daily 10:30 am to 3:30 pm (every hr. on the half hr.)

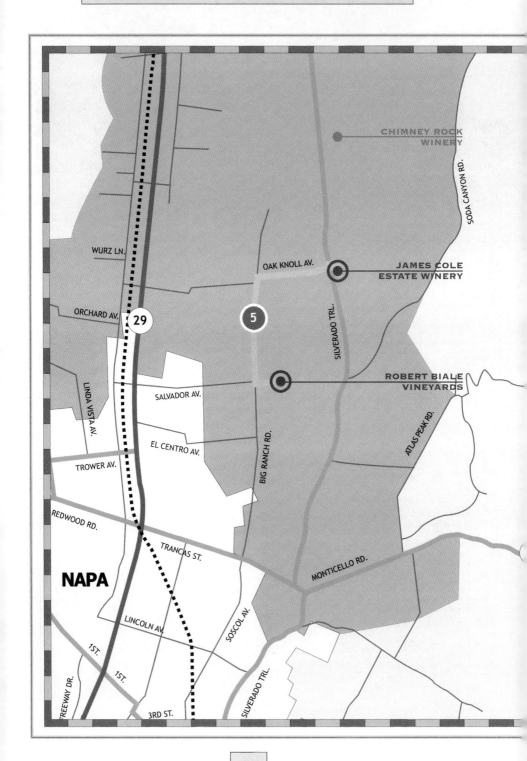

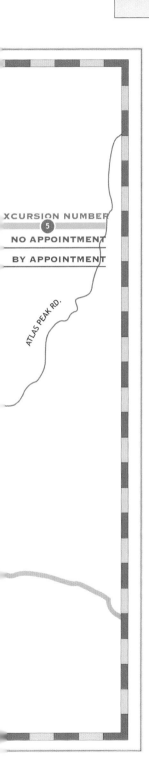

XCURSION NUMBER
5
NO APPOINTMENT
BY APPOINTMENT

ATLAS PEAK RD.

5

BIALE TO COLE

From Zinfandels & More to Cabernets Plus:

Your visit to the Biale and James Cole wineries both require that you make an appointment.

Robert Biale Vineyards: Allow at least an hour for Robert Biale Vineyards. No tours are offered here, just tastings. You may sip your wine on the back patio and don't hesitate to ask permission to wander off into the vineyard and sample grapes off the vine. The tasting consists of a flight of four to five wines. Biale produces between 9,000 and 10,000 cases annually. The staff are very friendly and the experience is a nice change from the group treatment typical of the big wineries. All of Biale's wines are good but it is famous for its Zinfandels so, if available, be sure to sample the Black Chicken or Aldo's Vineyard Zinfandels both of which are particularly notable.

James Cole Estate Winery: James Cole Estate Winery produces a 100% Cabernet Sauvignon estate block wine and a richer and more complex "Umbral" Reserve Cabernet. It also produces a Malbec, a Petit Verdot and an unusual dessert wine called "Jaden" Riesling Ice Wine from Canadian grapes harvested in the Okanagan Valley of British Columbia. Cole only produces about 98 cases of this sweet wine annually. The tasting room here, open until 5 pm, is welcoming and intimate. The staff are friendly, personable and knowledgeable. The consensus is that while James Cole's wines are not cheap, they are delicious and worth the price. Because the winery is small and quantities limited, it does not distribute, so purchases are only available at the winery.

Robert Biale Vineyards

Aldo Biale passed away on December 12, 2009. It was he and his son, Robert, who were responsible for putting together the partnership that was to become Robert Biale Vineyards. Aldo grew up on the family farm raising chickens and growing walnuts, prunes and Zinfandel grapes. To supplement the meager income from the ranch, Aldo made wine from the Zinfandel grapes on the property and sold it as "Black Chicken", a code name to conceal the fact that he was making wine illegally. Years later he and his son Robert decided to use those old Zinfandel vines to make a high end Zinfandel, a rarity in the Napa Valley where Cabernet Sauvignon was king. Aldo and Robert combined their own accumulated vineyard management knowledge with the marketing expertise of Dave Pramuk and the winemaking skills of Al Perry to form Robert Biale Vineyards in 1991. They specialized in Zinfandel but expanded into Petit Sirah, Syrah, Sangiovese, Barbera, Rhone blends and Sauvignon Blanc. Today, despite some changes in the composition of the partnership, all of Biale's wines, especially their Zinfandels, continue to be highly regarded. If you visit, be sure to try their Black Chicken Zin!

ROBERT BIALE VINEYARDS	
WEBSITE:	www.robertbialevineyards.com
TASTING:	$$/4 tastes
APPOINTMENT:	Required 1 hr. in advance weekdays, 24 hr. for weekends
ADDRESS:	4038 Big Ranch Road,
	Napa, CA 94558-1405
PHONE:	(707) 257-7555
HOURS:	Daily, 10 am - 4 pm
TOURS:	No tours

James Cole Estate Winery

James Cole Estate Winery takes its name from its owner-operators, the husband and wife team of James Harder and Colleen (aka Cole) Harder.

Colleen is from Whittier, California, and has a background in direct marketing with a focus on financial services. James, a Canadian, comes to the table with a history of sales and marketing expertise in the wine industry. He and two friends started their own company, Nine North Wines, and have since been busy producing wines from various parts of the Napa Valley. He and Colleen purchased 11 acres just off the Silverado Trail in 2000 and opened their James Cole Estate Winery tasting room in October of 2007.

Visits are by appointment only. This winery gets consistently high ratings from its visitors and earns high praise for its wine and tasting room staff. Although there are no formal tours, staff members are not adverse to showing guests around if time permits. The winery is small and produces approximately 1,200 cases of wine annually.

JAMES COLE ESTATE WINERY	
WEBSITE:	www.jamescolewinery.com
TASTING:	**$$**/4 tastes Signature, **$$$**/6 tastes Reserve Tasting
APPOINTMENT:	Required 1 hr. in advance for Mon-Thurs, 24 hrs. for Fri-Sun
ADDRESS:	5014 Silverado Trail,
	Napa, CA 94558
PHONE:	(707) 251-9905
HOURS:	Daily, 10 am - 5 pm
TOURS:	No formal tours

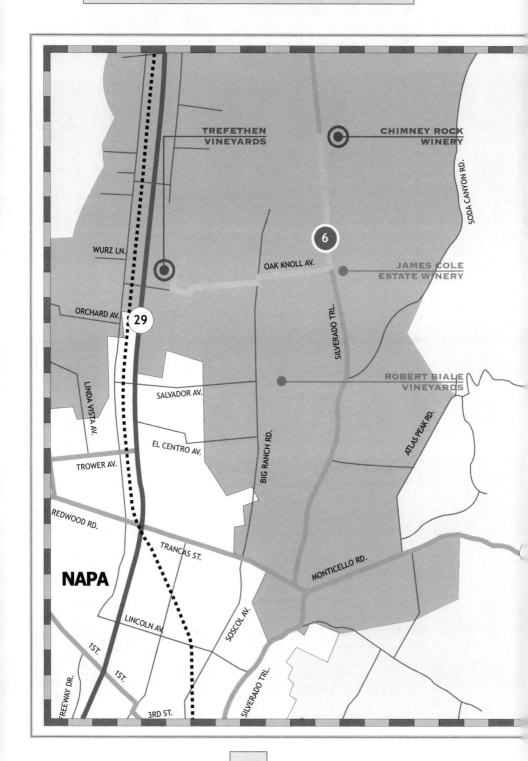

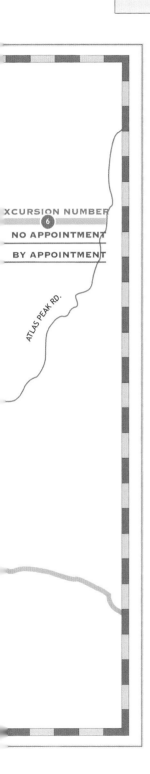

XCURSION NUMBER
6
NO APPOINTMENT
BY APPOINTMENT

ATLAS PEAK RD.

6

TREFETHEN TO CHIMNEY ROCK

From Oak Knoll to Stags Leap:

Trefethen Vineyards: Housed in the old restored Eshcol winery built in 1886, the large but cozy Trefethen Family Vineyards tasting room offers a comfortable tasting experience with a shared table on one end and scattered club chairs at the other. Pay your tasting fee at the front desk then proceed to the mini bar or be seated to be served at a table. The Estate Tasting consists of four wines and the Reserve Tasting includes five. There are no facilities for picnics. A 30-minute tour and tasting is offered at 10 am but reservations are required. Their Dry Riesling, Chardonnay, Viognier and Quandary (a blend of all three whites), are very popular as are their Cabernets, Cab Franc and Dragon's Tooth (a Malbec-based blend). Try the Late Harvest Riesling for dessert or HaLo for a Cabernet splurge.

Chimney Rock Winery: Chimney Rock Winery offers a 1 pm *Discover* tour and tasting Monday through Friday. A more in-depth *Behind the Scenes* tour is also offered daily at 11 am. Reservations for both are required. Chimney Rock's tasting room reflects an exterior Cape Dutch architectural influence with an interior high vaulted ceiling and a tasting bar in the middle. You may taste inside or feel free to enjoy your tasting on the back patio with umbrellaed tables and a calming ornamental water feature. There are several options for tasting four to five wines all of which fall within a *moderate* to *elevated* price range. The Cabernets from this Stags Leap winery should not be missed. Also try their *Elevage* and *Elevage Blanc* Bordeaux blends.

Trefethen Family Vineyards

Eugene Trefethen worked as an executive for Kaiser Industries building Hoover Dam and the San Francisco-Oakland Bay Bridge. On his retirement in 1968 he and his wife purchased 600 acres in the Napa Valley and began growing and selling grapes. Their son John, and his wife Janet, expanded the business and in 1973 produced Trefethen Vineyards' first commercial wine. Today Trefethen Vineyards remains a family business with all members participating in various aspects of production and marketing.

Trefethen's wines are produced from grapes grown solely on their own Oak Knoll property which encompasses 63 distinct vineyard blocks and nine different grape varieties. Each block is characterized by its own soil type, trellising system and irrigation plan all designed to maximize the potential for each grape variety.

Trefethen's tasting room is located in the historic Eshcol winery constructed by Hamden McIntyre in 1886. Having fallen into disrepair, John and Janet Trefethen have since restored the building to its former glory.

TREFETHEN FAMILY VINEYARDS	
WEBSITE:	www.trefethen.com
TASTING:	**$$**/4 tastes Estate Tasting, **$$**/5 tastes Reserve Tasting
APPOINTMENT:	Required for tours, special tastings and for groups of 7 or more
ADDRESS:	1160 Oak Knoll Avenue,
	Napa, CA 94558-1303
PHONE:	1+(866) 895-7696 or (707) 255-7700
HOURS:	Daily, 10 am - 4:30 pm
TOURS:	**$$**/daily 30-min. tour & tasting, 10 am by appointment

Chimney Rock Winery

The Chimney Rock Cape Dutch architecture harkens back to the time founder Sheldon "Hack" Wilson and his wife, Stella, spent in South Africa running Pepsi Cola. The Wilsons acquired Chimney Rock golf course in the Stags Leap District of Napa Valley in 1980 and promptly converted the first nine holes to growing grapes. They completed construction of their winery in 1989 with the hope of making wine comparable to the best produced in Bordeaux. Although the winery changed hands in 2004 and the Terlato family assumed sole ownership, the goal of making fine wine remained the same. Chimney Rock was added to the family's roster of wineries which included Rutherford Hill, Sanford, Alderbrook and their namesake Terlato Family Vineyards.

The winery produced its first vintage in 1984 and by 1990 had produced its first *Elevage*, a Bordeaux-style blend of Merlot, Cabernet Sauvignon and Cabernet Franc. In 2004 Chimney Rock produced its first *Elevage Blanc*, a Bordeaux-style blend of Sauvignon Blanc and Sauvignon Gris. Both *Elevage* and *Elevage Blanc* aspire to match the best of France's Chateau Haut-Brion and Chateau Haut-Brion Blanc.

CHIMNEY ROCK WINERY	
WEBSITE:	www.chimneyrock.com
TASTING:	Several basic tastings from **$$**/4-5 tastes to **$$$**/4 tastes
APPOINTMENT:	Required for tours and for groups of 8 or more
ADDRESS:	5350 Silverado Trail,
	Napa, CA 94558
PHONE:	1+(800) 257-2641, or (707) 257-2641 ext. 3218
HOURS:	Daily, 10 am - 5 pm
TOURS:	**$$$$**/Tours & Tastings, 11 am daily & 1 pm (M - F) by appt.

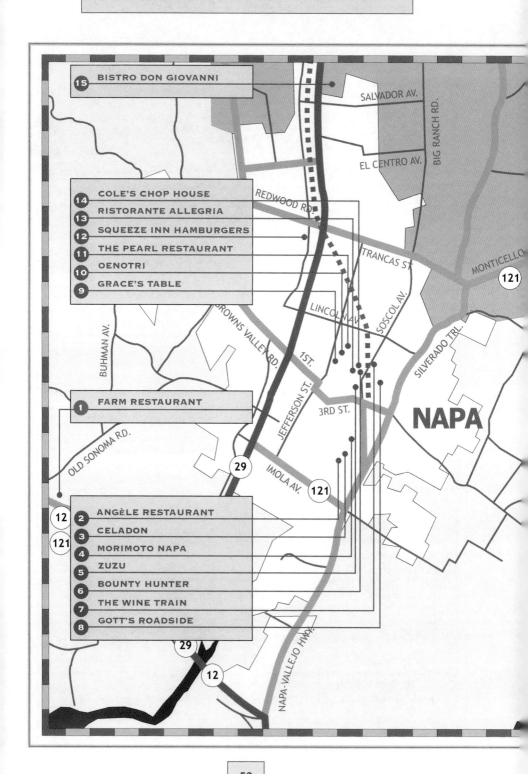

15 BISTRO DON GIOVANNI

14 COLE'S CHOP HOUSE
13 RISTORANTE ALLEGRIA
12 SQUEEZE INN HAMBURGERS
11 THE PEARL RESTAURANT
10 OENOTRI
9 GRACE'S TABLE

1 FARM RESTAURANT

2 ANGÈLE RESTAURANT
3 CELADON
4 MORIMOTO NAPA
5 ZUZU
6 BOUNTY HUNTER
7 THE WINE TRAIN
8 GOTT'S ROADSIDE

NAPA

RESTAURANTS:
LOWER
NAPA
VALLEY

KEY:	Restaurant Ratings	
		RESTAURANTS **xx**
OVERALL QUALITY		**COST PER PERSON**
		Under $10............................($)
Good:	★★★☆☆	$10 - $30.............................($$)
Superior:	★★★★☆	$31 - $60.............................($$$)
Exceptional:	★★★★★	Above $60..........................($$$$)

LOWER NAPA VALLEY RESTAURANTS

FARM: The Carneros Inn, 4048 Sonoma Hwy., Napa CA 94559
rating: ★★★★☆
hours: W-Sun, 5:30 pm -10 pm (dinner menu)
      Daily, 4 pm -10 pm (bar & pavilion menu)
website: www.thecarnerosinn.com/pj_farm.html
category: New American

(707) 299-4880
price: **($$$)**

1

ANGÈLE: 540 Main St., St Helena, CA 94559
rating: ★★★★☆
hours: Sun - Th, 11:30 am - 9 pm
      F - Sat, 11:30 am - 10 pm
website: www.angelerestaurant.com
category: French

(707) 252-8115
price: **($$$)**

2

CELADON: 500 Main St., Napa CA 94559
rating: ★★★★☆
hours: M - F, 11:30 am - 2:30 pm (lunch menu)
      M - F, 2:30 pm - 5 pm (afternoon menu) & Daily, 5 pm - 9 pm (dinner)
website: www.celadonnapa.com
category: New American

(707) 254-9690
price: **($$$)**

3

MORIMOTO NAPA: 610 Main St., Napa CA 94559
rating: ★★★★☆
hours: M - Thu, Sun 11:30 am - 12 am
      Fri - Sat, 11:30 am - 1 am
website: www.morimotonapa.com
category: Asian Fusion, Japanese, Sushi

(707) 252-1600
price: **($$$$)**

4

ZUZU: 829 Main St., Napa CA 94559
rating: ★★★★☆
hours: M - Thu, 11:30 am - 10 pm   F, 11:30 am - 11 pm
      Sat, 4 pm - 11 pm   Sun, 4 pm - 9:30 pm
website: www.zuzunapa.com
category: Tapas, Spanish

(707) 224-8555
price: **($$)**

5

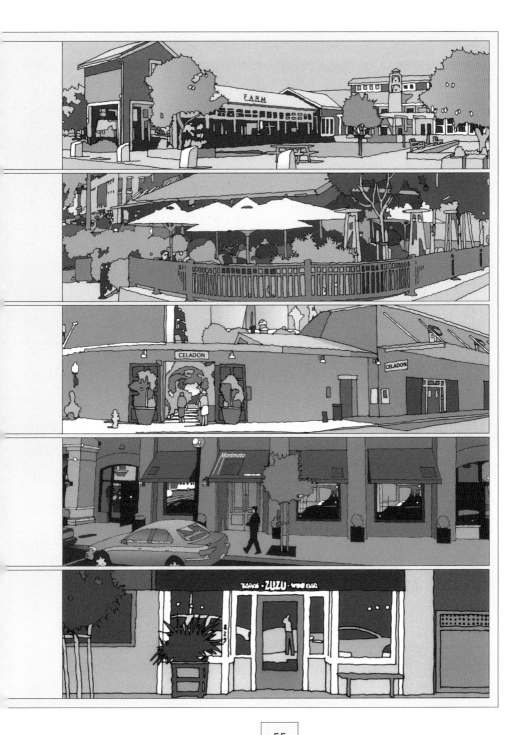

LOWER NAPA VALLEY RESTAURANTS

BOUNTY HUNTER WINE BAR & SMOKIN' BBQ: 975 1st St., Napa CA 94559
rating: ★★★★☆
(707) 226-3976
hours: M-Th & Sun, 11 am -10 pm
price: **($$)**
   F-Sat, 11 am -12 pm
website: www.bountyhunterwinebar.com
category: Barbecue, Wine Bar

6

WINE TRAIN: 1275 McKinstry St., Napa CA 94559
rating: ★★★⯪☆
(707) 253-2111
hours: M - Sun, 8 am - 6 pm
price: **($$$$)**
website: www.winetrain.com
category: New American

7

GOTT'S ROADSIDE: The Oxbow Public Market, 644 1st. St., Napa CA 94559
rating: ★★★★☆
(707) 224-6900
hours: M - Sun, 10:30 am - 9 pm (winter)
price: **($$)**
   M - Sun, 10:30 am - 10 pm (summer)
website: http://gotts.com
category: Burgers

8

GRACE'S TABLE: 1400 2nd. St., Napa CA 94559
rating: ★★★★☆
(707) 226-6200
hours: M-Th, 8:30 am - 9:00 pm
price: **($$)**
   F-Sat, 8:30 am - 10:00 pm   Sun, 10:00 am - 9:00 pm
website: www.gracestable.net.com
category: New American

9

OENOTRI: 1425 1st St., Napa 94559
rating: ★★★★☆
(707) 252-1022
hours: M-F, 11:30 am - 2:30 pm (lunch)
price: **($$$)**
   Sun-Th, 5:30 pm - 9:30 pm   F-Sat, 5:30 pm -10 pm (dinner)
website: www.oenotri.com
category: Italian

10

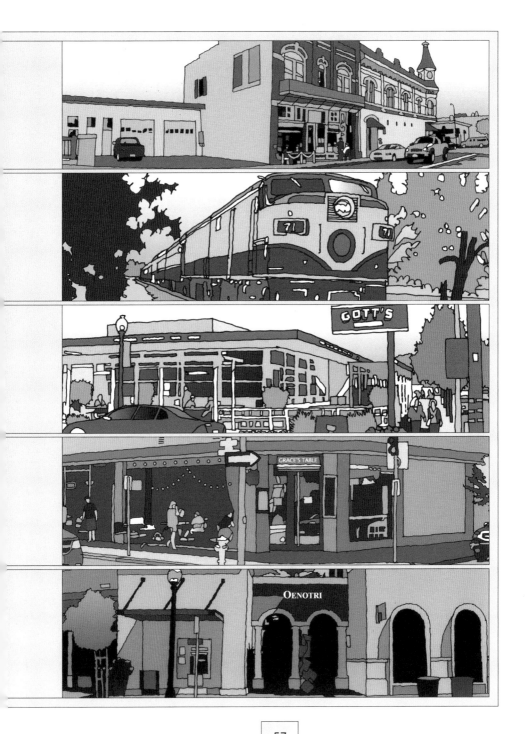

LOWER NAPA VALLEY RESTAURANTS

THE PEARL RESTAURANT: 1339 Pearl St. Ste. 104, Napa CA 94559
rating: ★★★★☆   (707) 224-8555
hours: Tu-Sat, 11:30 am - 2 pm (lunch)   price: **($$)**
        Tu-Th, 5:30 pm - 9 pm   F-Sat, 5:30 pm - 9:30 pm (dinner)
website: www.therestaurantpearl.com
category: New American   **11**

SQUEEZE INN HAMBURGERS: 3383 Solano Ave., Napa 94558
rating: ★★★★☆   (707) 257-6880
hours: M - F, 11 am - 8 pm   price: **($)**
        Sat,   11 am - 7 pm   Sun, closed
website: www.squeezeinnhamburgers.com
category: Burgers   **12**

RISTORANTE ALLEGRIA: 1026 1st. St., Napa CA 94558
rating: ★★★★☆   (707) 224-8555
hours: M - Sun, 11:30 am - 2:30 pm (lunch)   price: **($$)**
        M - Sun, 5 pm - closing (dinner), (F - Sun, no closure 2:30 pm - 5 pm)
website: www.ristoranteallegria.com
category: Italian   **13**

COLE'S CHOP HOUSE: 1122 Main St., Napa CA 94559
rating: ★★★★☆   (707) 224-6328
hours: Sun - Th, 5 pm - 9 pm   price: **($$$$)**
        F - Sat, 5 pm - 10 pm
website: www.coleschophouse.com
category: Steakhouse   **14**

BISTRO DON GIOVANNI: 4110 Howard Ln., Napa CA 94558
rating: ★★★★☆   (707) 224-3300
hours: Sun - Th, 11:30 am - 10 pm   price: **($$$)**
        F - Sat, 11:30 am - 11 pm
website: www.bistrodongiovanni.com
category: Italian   **15**

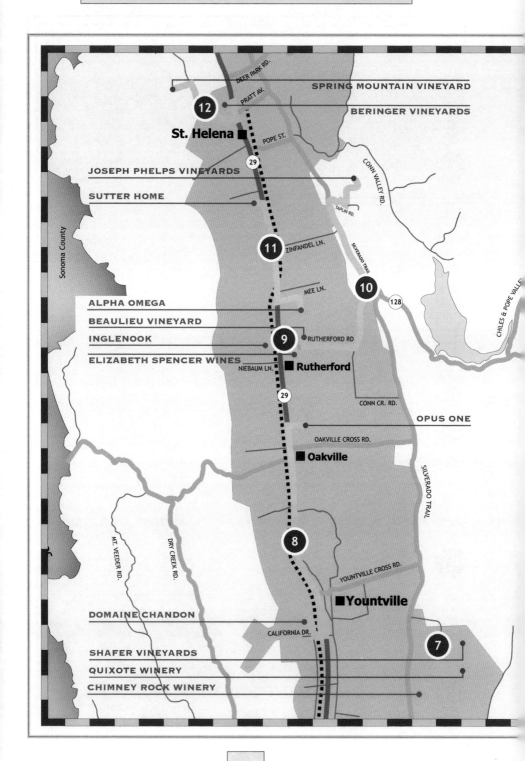

DEER PARK RD.

PRATT AV.

SPRING MOUNTAIN VINEYARD

BERINGER VINEYARDS

12

St. Helena ■

POPE ST.

CONN VALLEY RD.

29

JOSEPH PHELPS VINEYARDS

SUTTER HOME

TAPLIN RD.

11 ZINFANDEL LN.

SILVERADO TRAIL

MEE LN.

10

128

CHILES & POPE VALLEY

ALPHA OMEGA

BEAULIEU VINEYARD

INGLENOOK

9 RUTHERFORD RD

ELIZABETH SPENCER WINES

NIEBAUM LN. ■ **Rutherford**

29

CONN CR. RD.

OPUS ONE

OAKVILLE CROSS RD.

■ **Oakville**

SILVERADO TRAIL

8

YOUNTVILLE CROSS RD.

■ **Yountville**

DOMAINE CHANDON

MT. VEEDER RD.

DRY CREEK RD.

CALIFORNIA DR.

7

SHAFER VINEYARDS

QUIXOTE WINERY

CHIMNEY ROCK WINERY

Sonoma County

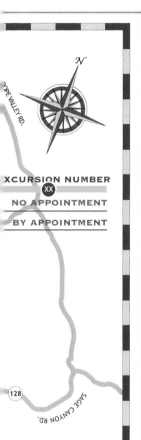

MID NAPA VALLEY:

Six Day-Trips to Twelve Mid Valley Wineries

From Quixote Winery to
Spring Mountain Vineyard

KEY:	Winery Guide	
Green: NO APPOINTMENT		**Red: BY APPOINTMENT**
COST PER PERSON		
Nominal.......(0 - $14)..........**$**		
Moderate.....($15 - $29).....**$$**		
Elevated.......($30 - $44).....**$$$**		
Spendy.........($45 PLUS).....**$$$$**		

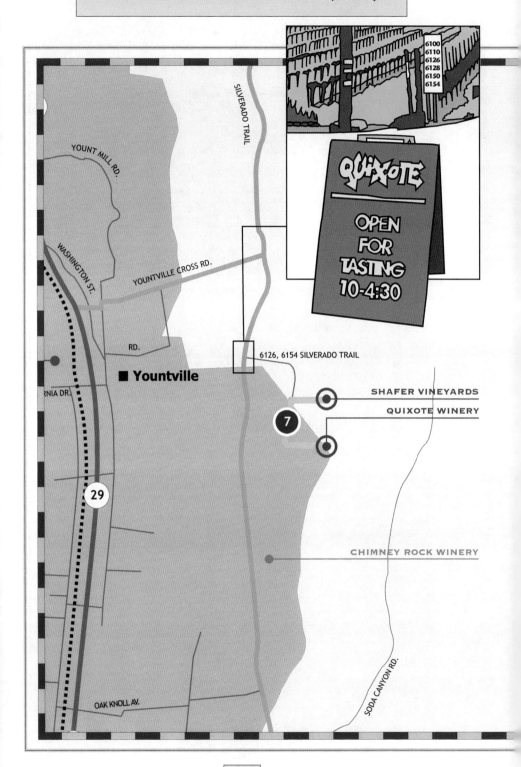

6100
6110
6126
6128
6150
6154

QUIXOTE

OPEN FOR TASTING 10-4:30

SILVERADO TRAIL

YOUNT MILL RD.

WASHINGTON ST.

YOUNTVILLE CROSS RD.

RD.

■ Yountville

RNIA DR.

6126, 6154 SILVERADO TRAIL

SHAFER VINEYARDS

QUIXOTE WINERY

7

29

CHIMNEY ROCK WINERY

SODA CANYON RD.

OAK KNOLL AV.

XCURSION NUMBER
7

NO APPOINTMENT

BY APPOINTMENT

7

QUIXOTE TO SHAFER

Two Stags Leap Wineries:

These wineries can be a little tricky to find. Look for the side road marked by a sign with several stacked addresses (6126, 6154 etc.) off to the right as you proceed north on the Silverado Trail. Quixote often marks the turn with a sandwich board. Both wineries also require appointments.

Quixote Winery: Quixote Winery is literally within view of Shafer and offers tours and tastings daily, except Mondays. Book a noon appointment at Quixote then follow it with the 2 pm Shafer tasting. Arrange your Shafer appointment first as its reservation lead time can be somewhat lengthy. Visits to Quixote on the other hand can often be arranged within hours of your anticipated arrival. Allow between 60 and 75 minutes for your tour and tasting. The Hundertwasser designed building and tasting room are the undeniable focal points of this winery.

Shafer Vineyards: Shafer Vineyards tastings are given at 10 am and 2 pm, Monday through Friday. Depending on the time of year, appointments must be made anywhere from one to as much as six weeks in advance. The tasting consists of a 90-minute tasting-tutorial. There is no winery tour as such. A tasting docent will lead you through a brief history of the winery and information about each of the five wines you taste, including their flagship Hillside Select Cabernet. The tasting is conducted in a comfortable, sit-down, living-room style environment overlooking the patio and vineyards with a group consisting of no more than 10 people.

Quixote Winery

Carl Doumani purchased Stags' Leap Winery in 1972. After 25 years of operation he sold it to Beringer Wine Estates. In 1996 he founded Quixote Winery on adjacent property as a boutique winery devoted exclusively to making small quantities of Petite Sirah and Cabernet Sauvignon under the flagship "Quixote" and secondary "Panza" labels. Quixote Winery produces about 3,000 cases annually utilizing state-of-the-art organic farming techniques.

The winery itself was designed by Austrian painter-architect Friedensreich Hundertwasser. He is known for his use of bold colors, irregular forms and for his incorporation of natural landscape features. The project took 10 years to complete.

Quixote is in the vanguard of a growing number of wine producers exploring the use of twist-top closures to reduce spoilage or "corked" wine. Additionally, twist-top closures allow wine to be stored vertically keeping sediment at the bottom of the bottle obviating the need to stand them upright for hours before opening.

QUIXOTE WINERY	
WEBSITE:	www.quixotewinery.com
TASTING:	**$$**/4 tastes & tour
APPOINTMENT:	Required, by phone or email "Info@quixotewinery.com"
ADDRESS:	6126 Silverado Trail,
	Napa, CA 94558
PHONE:	(707) 944-2659
HOURS:	10 am - 4:30 pm (closed Mon.)
TOURS:	60 min. at 10 am, 12 pm, 2 pm (and 4 pm May-Oct)

Shafer Vineyards

John Shafer began Shafer Vineyards in 1972 after a 23-year career in publishing. He crushed his first Cabernet grapes in 1978 and began construction of a winery a year later. John's son, Doug became the winemaker in 1983 after graduating from U.C. Davis. Ten years later, John became chairman-of-the-board, Doug moved into the president's position overseeing daily operations as well as sales and marketing, and the winemaker duties fell to Doug's assistant winemaker and longtime friend, Elias Fernandez.

The uniqueness of the Stags Leap district is characterized by Cabernets with rich fruit and soft tannins. Shafer's flagship wine is its Hillside Select Cabernet. The 2006 vintage consists of 100% Cabernet fruit and retails for $215 per bottle.

In addition to 50 acres in the Stags Leap District, Shafer has expanded to over 200 acres with additional vineyards in the Carneros and Oak Knoll districts. It annually produces about 34,000 cases consisting of Cabernet Sauvignon, Merlot, Chardonnay, Sangiovese and Syrah.

SHAFER VINEYARDS	
WEBSITE:	*www.shafervineyards.com*
TASTING:	***$$$$**/5 tastes*
APPOINTMENT:	*Required, sometimes as much as 1 to 6 weeks in advance*
ADDRESS:	*6154 Silverado Trail,*
	Napa, CA 94558
PHONE:	*(707) 944-2877 or info@shafervineyards.com*
HOURS:	*9 am - 4 pm (Mon - Fri), closed weekends*
TOURS:	*Sit-down tasting only, 10 am & 2 pm (weekdays only)*

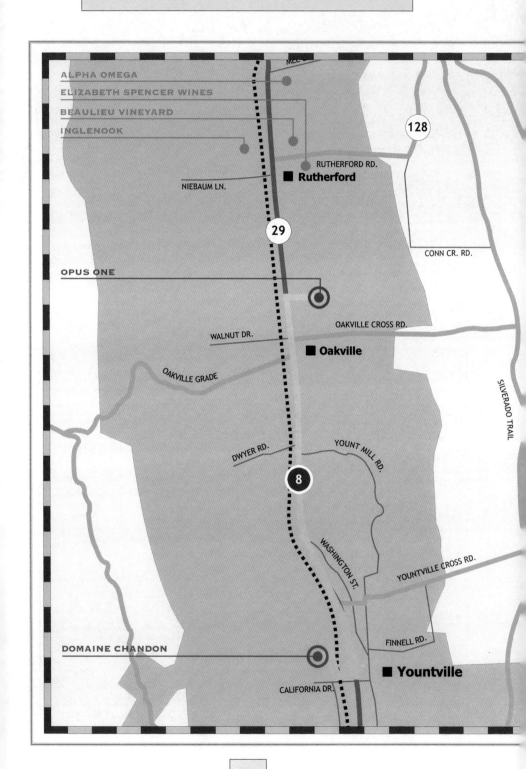

ALPHA OMEGA
ELIZABETH SPENCER WINES
BEAULIEU VINEYARD
INGLENOOK

MILL

128

RUTHERFORD RD.
■ Rutherford

NIEBAUM LN.

29

CONN CR. RD.

OPUS ONE

OAKVILLE CROSS RD.

WALNUT DR.

■ Oakville

OAKVILLE GRADE

SILVERADO TRAIL

DWYER RD.

YOUNT MILL RD.

8

WASHINGTON ST.

YOUNTVILLE CROSS RD.

FINNELL RD.

DOMAINE CHANDON

■ Yountville

CALIFORNIA DR.

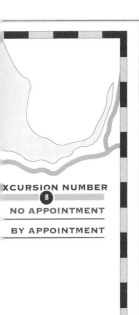

XCURSION NUMBER
8
NO APPOINTMENT
BY APPOINTMENT

8

CHANDON TO OPUS ONE

Sparkling Wine and Proprietary Blends :

Domaine Chandon: Begin this excursion around noon with a visit to Domaine Chandon's tasting room where you may sample flights of wine or simply order a bottle to enjoy on the patio. Take in the scenery at the winery, enjoy the featured artwork in the lobby and browse the gift shop. If you'd like a tour, you should begin about 45 minutes earlier with one of the late-morning tours. These tours should allow plenty of time for you to squeeze in Opus One's 1:30 pm or 2:30 pm *Estate Tour* should you wish to take it as well. Tours and schedules at Domaine Chandon change frequently so be sure to check ahead to confirm what's offered and at what times. There are currently three 90-minute tours available which are offered throughout the day on a daily basis. Reservations are recommended but not required for groups of 9 or less.

Opus One: Continue your wine-tasting excursion with a ten-minute drive to Opus One. Tastings and tours require an appointment. The afternoon *Estate Tour* is offered at 1:30 pm and 2:30 pm, includes a tasting and lasts about 90 minutes. If you're not interested in a tour and would rather just do a tasting, samples are offered in the Partner's Room and consist of one pour of the current release and, when available, a sample of one additional vintage. Opus One's wines are said to be so expensive due to the enormous amount of labor-intensive work involved in their making. It is ranked as one of the most expensive single product facilities in the world.

Domaine Chandon

Domaine Chandon was launched in 1973 by its parent company, Moët-Hennessy, as the first French owned sparkling wine producer in California. It was the first California winery to use only Napa Valley Pinot Noir and Chardonnay for all of its premium quality sparkling wines. The winery has 1,000 acres of vineyards in various Napa Valley appellations including Los Carneros, Mt. Veeder and Yountville. Domaine Chandon is unique in having a Michelin-starred restaurant, *étoile*, located on its property as well. The winery is renowned for its Brut and Brut Classic sparkling wines. It also produces still wines: Chardonnay, Pinot Noir and Pinot Meunier.

Moët Chandon is one of the world's largest champagne producers and prominent champagne houses. Jas Hennessy & Co. is a leading cognac producer. Louis Vuitton is a purveyor of status symbol fashion luxury goods. The merger of these companies gave rise to *Moët Hennessy•Louis Vuitton* or *LVMH*. Napa Valley's Domaine Chandon operates as one of about 60 largely autonomous subsidiaries of this conglomerate.

DOMAINE CHANDON

WEBSITE:	www.chandon.com
TASTING:	**$$**/4 tastes Classic, **$$**/3 tastes Reserve, Varietal & Prestige
APPOINTMENT:	Required for groups of 10 or more and for some tours & tastings
ADDRESS:	1 California Drive,
	Yountville, CA 94599
PHONE:	1+(888) 242-6366 or (707) 204-7461
HOURS:	Daily, 10 am - 5 pm (closed major holidays)
TOURS:	**$$$**/various daily tours, (check website for offerings)

Opus One

Opus One makes and releases only one wine per vintage: a world class proprietary Bordeaux-style blend. It began in 1979 with the production of the first vintage by winemakers Lucien Signneau and Timothy Mondavi as a joint venture between wine industry giants Baron Philippe de Rothschild and Robert Mondavi. By 1984 Opus One had become known for having established a category of ultra-premium wine priced at $50 per bottle and above. Today, the 2006 vintage of Opus One is rated 93 points by Robert Parker's *The Wine Advocate* and is priced between $270 and $350 per bottle.

Opus One's unique and elegant winery was constructed in 1991. It features a roof-top terrace where you can enjoy both a glass of wine and expansive views of the valley's vineyards. Tastings of the current and, occasionally, an additional vintage are available in the Partner's Room. A 90-minute winery tour, including a tasting, is also available. Whether it's the tasting or one of the tours you opt for, remember all require a reservation which you may make by calling 1+(800) 292-6787.

OPUS ONE	
WEBSITE:	www.opusonewinery.com
TASTING:	$$$/1 taste current release and one additional vintage if available
APPOINTMENT:	Required
ADDRESS:	7900 St. Helena Hwy.,
	Oakville, CA 94562
PHONE:	1+(800) 292-6787 or (707) 944-9442
HOURS:	Daily, 10 am - 4 pm (last tasting at 3:30 pm)
TOURS:	$$$$/Estate Tour or $$$$/Double Vintage Tour & Tasting

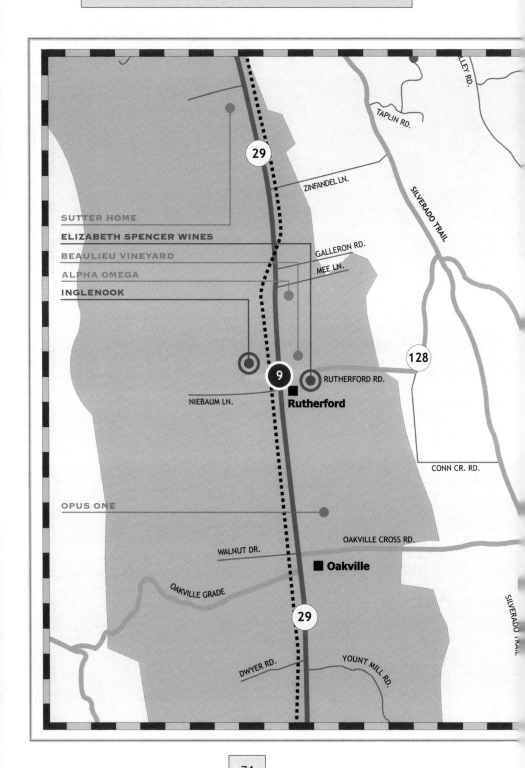

XCURSION NUMBER

9

NO APPOINTMENT

BY APPOINTMENT

9

SPENCER TO INGLENOOK

Tasting Room to Chateau Room:

Elizabeth Spencer Wines: The Elizabeth Spencer Wines tasting room is a gem just a little off the beaten path directly opposite Beaulieu Vineyard. If you're having lunch at the Rutherford Grill, it's located across the street in the old brick post office building. Wander over for the Charter Tasting which is a flight of four wines and, sometimes, a bonus wine. You may taste inside the small 14-person tasting room or have your tasting in the adjoining courtyard for a slight additional charge. It is a relaxing and pleasant way to spend the afternoon. The staff are friendly and informative, the wines are good and the pours are generous. Although small, this is a refreshing change to the often impersonal nature of the large wineries.

Inglenook: After Elizabeth Spencer, venture across Highway 29, opposite the Rutherford Grill, to Francis Ford Coppola's Inglenook. Tasting and tour options change so frequently at this winery that you really have to consult their website or call ahead to verify their offerings. There are a variety of tour and tasting experiences or just tastings available. Most require a reservation. The Heritage Tasting of four wines is given tableside in the Pennino Salon with baguette and cheese and requires reservations. But you are welcome to drop by the Bistro for a sampling of three wines with no appointment needed. You may sample your wine in a casual cafe setting either inside or outdoors overlooking the fountain. You're also invited to browse through the artifacts and memorabilia of the Centennial Museum.

Elizabeth Spencer Wines

Elizabeth Spencer is located in what was formerly the old Rutherford post office. There is no winery here, just a charming little tasting room and outdoor patio. Their grapes are sourced from a "handful of dedicated growers and a dozen vineyard blocks" and then made into wine at a custom crush facility. Their Cabernet Sauvignon comes from select Napa Valley vineyards while the Chardonnay, Pinot Noir and Syrah come from the Sonoma Coast. In 2005 they produced small quantities of Napa Valley Chardonnay, Mendocino Sauvignon Blanc, and Sonoma Coast Rosé of Syrah.

Elizabeth Pressler has an extensive background in the wine industry and Spencer Graham's background is in food and wine. They married and Elizabeth Spencer became a reality in 1988.

Reservations are requested but not required for the Charter and Library Tastings. They consist of four wines and, occasionally, a bonus. Reservations are required 48 hours in advance for additional or special tastings.

ELIZABETH SPENCER WINES	
WEBSITE:	www.elizabethspencerwines.com
TASTING:	$$/4 tastes Charter, $$$/4 tastes Library
APPOINTMENT:	Required for special tastings
ADDRESS:	1165 Rutherford Road,
	Rutherford, CA 94573
PHONE:	(707) 963-4762 or (707) 963-6067
HOURS:	Daily, 10 am - 6 pm
TOURS:	No tours. See website for additional tastings, $$$ to $$$$.

Inglenook

Inglenook was founded in 1880 by Gustave Niebaum. Within only ten years he managed to garner international acclaim for his wines. In post-Prohibition years, the Inglenook legacy was continued under Niebaum's wife's grand-nephew, John Daniel. Film director Francis Ford Coppola acquired the winery in 1975 and began making wine under the Niebaum-Coppola Estate label. In 2006, having reacquired all of the vineyards originally held by Inglenook and having returned winemaking to the Chateau, Niebaum-Coppola became Rubicon Estate. Today, in addition to the winery, the restored Chateau contains two tasting rooms, a wine bar, a museum with wine and film artifacts and a retail sales shop. To mark the restoration of the property to its original state, the Inglenook trademark was purchased in 2011 and Rubicon Estate was renamed Inglenook.

Among the wines Inglenook produces are *Rubicon*, their flagship Bordeaux-style blend, *Blancaneaux*, their flagship Rhone-style white wine blend and *CASK Cabernet*, a tribute to the Cabernet Sauvignons originally made by John Daniel.

INGLENOOK	
WEBSITE:	*www.inglenook.com*
TASTING:	*$$/3 tastes Bistro (no appt.), $$$$/4 tastes Heritage (by appt.)*
APPOINTMENT:	*Required for groups of 9 or more and for special tours & tastings*
ADDRESS:	*1991 St. Helena Hwy,*
	Rutherford, CA 94573
PHONE:	*1+(800) 782-4266 or (707) 968-1100 or (707) 968-1161*
HOURS:	*Daily, 10:00 am - 5 pm*
TOURS:	*$$$$/Check website for specific offerings and times.*

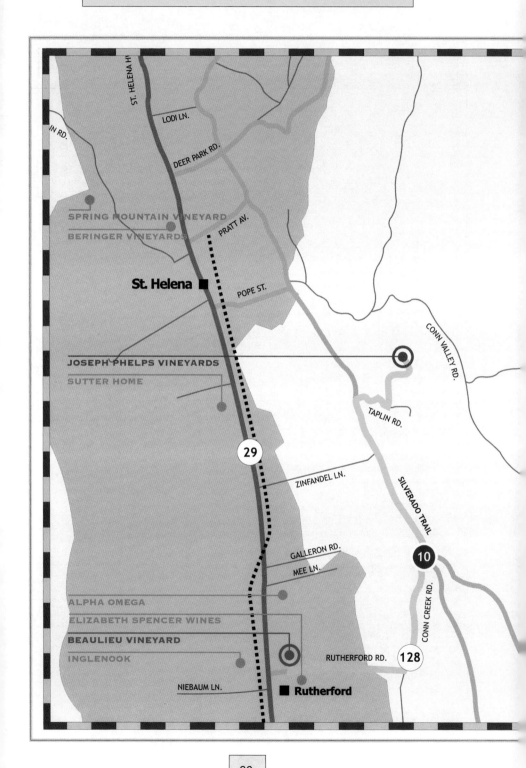

XCURSION NUMBER
10
NO APPOINTMENT
BY APPOINTMENT

10

BEAULIEU TO PHELPS

Rutherford to Spring Valley:

Beaulieu Vineyard: Start this trip around noon at Beaulieu Vineyard in Rutherford. No appointment is necessary for this winery if all you want to do is taste. Beaulieu offers a *Historic Tour and Barrel Tasting* which requires prior arrangement. Their basic tastings are offered in the BV Visitor Center where you are greeted at the door with a complimentary glass of wine. Don't forget to download the two-for-one tasting coupon usually available on their website. A four-wine Maestro Tasting and a four-wine Premier Tasting of Cabernets are offered. Although more expensive, you may opt for the Cabernet Reserve Tasting. These wines are of higher quality and include a tasting of the Georges de Latour Private Reserve. The drive to your next stop at Joseph Phelps should take about 15 minutes.

Joseph Phelps Vineyards: Joseph Phelps Vineyards closes at 5 pm on weekdays and at 4 pm on the weekend. All visits are by appointment. Its Terrace Tasting consists of six wines and includes its flagship wine, *Insignia*. The last Terrace Tasting starts at 3:30 pm during the week and 2:30 pm on the weekend. The tasting is self-paced and limited only by closing time. Arriving at Phelps around 2 pm allows you to participate in either of two Terrace Tasting options or one of their more formal and in-depth seminars. Seminars and private tastings require prior arrangement. Make this your last stop and just enjoy the view and setting until the winery closes or find your way back to where you started this trip and have an early dinner at the Rutherford Grill.

81

Beaulieu Vineyard

Beaulieu Vineyard, so the story goes, was named when Georges de Latour arrived in Rutherford with his wife, Fernande, and she exclaimed, "beau lieu" or "beautiful place." Thanks to its production of sacramental wine during Prohibition, it is one of the longest continuously operating wineries in the Napa Valley. Its founder, Georges de Latour, created the winery in 1900 and with his hiring of enologist and viticulturist Andre Tshelistcheff in 1936, introduced a new era of innovation to Napa Valley winemaking. Today Beaulieu is a leader in clonal research and a practitioner of sustainable farming techniques. Its vineyards cover more than 1,100 acres in the Napa Valley and in California's coastal growing regions.

BV's flagship wine and benchmark of Rutherford Cabernet is the Georges de Latour Private Reserve Cabernet Sauvignon, first bottled in 1936 by Andre Tshelistcheff. Other notables include Beaulieu Reserve Wines (expressions of BV's premier estates), BV Napa Valley Wines (from vineyards owned or leased in the Napa Valley), Beaulieu Vineyard Maestro Collection (available only at the winery) and BV Coastal Estates (priced, as they say, to be enjoyed daily).

BEAULIEU VINEYARD	
WEBSITE:	www.bvwines.com
TASTING:	**$$**/4 tastes Maestro, **$$**/4 tastes Premier, **$$$**/4 tastes Reserve
APPOINTMENT:	Required for special tastings and the Historic Tour
ADDRESS:	1960 St. Helena Hwy. South,
	Rutherford, CA 94573
PHONE:	1+(800) 373-5896 or (707) 967-5233
HOURS:	Daily, 10 am - 5 pm
TOURS:	**$$$**/Historic Tour & Barrel Tasting, 11 am & 2:30 pm (4 - 10 people)

Joseph Phelps Vineyards

Joseph Phelps purchased the 600 acre Spring Valley Connolly cattle ranch in 1973 and began planting vineyards. He was running a large construction company at the time and had just finished building what is today the Rutherford Hill Winery outside of St. Helena. Inspired by the area and looking to change his career, he constructed his own winery in 1974.

Joseph Phelps Vineyards' primary focus is on Bordeaux varietals and their flagship proprietary Bordeaux blend is *Insignia*, which has had at least 30 of its last vintages rated 90 or more by various prestigious wine publications. Other Phelps estate grown wines include Cabernet Sauvignon, Sauvignon Blanc, Viognier, Backus (a single vineyard Cabernet Sauvignon) and Elsrébe, a dessert wine from the Scheurebe grape. A small amount of Syrah is also produced from grapes sourced from a grower in the Carneros region of the Napa Valley. Additionally, Phelps crafts wine in their Freestone Winery, similar in style to wine made in Burgundy, from Chardonnay and Pinot Noir grapes grown on the Sonoma Coast.

JOSEPH PHELPS VINEYARDS	
WEBSITE:	www.jpvwines.com
TASTING:	**$$$**/6 tastes Terrace #1, **$$$$**/6 tastes Terrace Tasting #2
APPOINTMENT:	Required (6 guests per party limit for Terrace Tasting)
ADDRESS:	200 Taplin Road,
	St. Helena, CA 94574
PHONE:	1+(800) 707-5789 or (707) 967-3720
HOURS:	9 am - 5 pm (Mon - Fri) & 10 am - 4 pm (Sat - Sun)
TOURS:	No Tours (private tastings and seminars available)

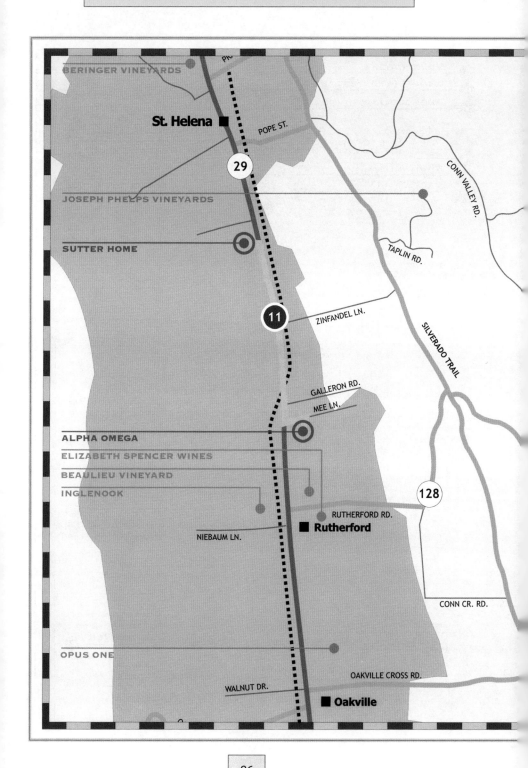

XCURSION NUMBER
11
NO APPOINTMENT
BY APPOINTMENT

11

ALPHA OMEGA TO SUTTER HOME

Boutique to Mass Market Winery:

This excursion is an exercise in contrasts in that it will take you from a modest 8,000 case winery to the tasting room of the nation's sixth largest wine producer: a 10 million case winery.

Alpha Omega: Alpha Omega opened in 2006 as a boutique winery and the response to its wines, its setting, the winery and its staff has been enthusiastic. While there is no formal tour, time permitting, the staff is happy to show guests through the winery for a quick look. Picnicking reservations are recommended and are available on a first come, first served basis during the week. Picnicking is available only for Wine Club Members on weekends and reservations are required. Tastings generally consist of four samples. You may have them inside at the bar or outside on the Terrace. Purchase a bottle and the tasting fee is refunded.

Sutter Home Family Vineyards: Sutter Home Family Vineyards offers a four-wine complimentary tasting. People who are just beginning to appreciate wine quite frequently start with sweeter wines and only later develop a taste for dry wines. Sutter Home is ideal for those individuals. While they produce dry wines, much of what they produce is mildly and pleasantly sweet. Try the Riesling, White Zinfandel, Moscato and Zinfandel Port. All of the wines are affordable and generally ideal when paired with everyday meals or just plain burgers. Although there is no winery tour offered, the tasting room is inviting, the servers are friendly and the adjoining garden is pleasant.

Alpha Omega

Established in July 2006 Alpha Omega is, by its own account, one of the valley's newest boutique wineries. Its grapes are sourced from a variety of notable vineyards located in various appellations throughout the Napa Valley. This makes for wines that are rich in complexity and aromatic profile. The goal of the winery's founders, Robin Baggett and Eric Sklar, is to make wines that combine an Old World European balanced style with New World fruit and tannins. Their flagship wine, *Era Napa Valley*, a blend of Bordeaux varietals, exemplifies this philosophy. Both their 2006 *Era* and 2007 Chardonnay received a 94 from the *Wine Spectator*. Be sure to sample their Cabernet Sauvignon, Proprietary Red, Rosé, Sauvignon Blanc and Late Harvest wines as well. Alpha Omega produces about 8,000 cases of wine annually.

Tastings usually consist of four wines. Private tastings may be arranged for groups of 10 to 100. Contact the events manager at (707) 302-1134. Private wine tastings for reserve wines and vertical tastings as well as wine and cheese tastings for four or more guests are also available by appointment.

ALPHA OMEGA	
WEBSITE:	www.aowinery.com
TASTING:	**$$**/4 tastes Standard, **$$$$**/4 tastes Reserve
APPOINTMENT:	Required for groups of 6 or more
ADDRESS:	1155 Mee Lane at Hwy 29,
	Rutherford, CA 94573
PHONE:	(707) 963-9999
HOURS:	Daily, 10 am - 6 pm
TOURS:	Nothing formal but will show you around if not busy.

Sutter Home Family Vineyards

In 1874 German-Swiss winemaker, John Thomann, established a small winery and distillery in the Napa Valley. Following his death, the winery was sold to another Swiss family, the Leunbergers, who actually named the estate Sutter Home. Shut down by Prohibition and abandoned until 1948, Sutter Home was resurrected by brothers, John and Mario Trinchero, who purchased the property and operated it as a small mom and pop family winery. In 1972 Mario's son, Bob Trinchero, having developed an interest in single-vineyard Zinfandels from Amador County, decided to explore the idea of White Zinfandel. By 1987 it had become the best selling premium wine in the United States. Of the approximately 10 million cases of White Zinfandel produced annually, Sutter Home is responsible for 45% of sales. Today, Sutter Home is the sixth largest winery in the United States and Trinchero Family Estates, which currently sells wine under 20 labels including Folie à Deux and Newman's Own, is the nation's second largest independent family-run winery. Visitors to Sutter Home are welcomed with free wine tasting and, while there is no winery tour, are encouraged to take a self-guided tour of the gardens.

SUTTER HOME FAMILY VINEYARDS	
WEBSITE:	www.sutterhome.com
TASTING:	$/4 tastes
APPOINTMENT:	Required for groups of 6 or more
ADDRESS:	277 St. Helena Hwy. (Hwy. 29),
	South St. Helena, CA 94574
PHONE:	1+(800) 967-4663 or (707) 963-3104 ext. 4208
HOURS:	Daily, 10 am - 5 pm
TOURS:	Self-guided tour of the White Zinfandel Garden

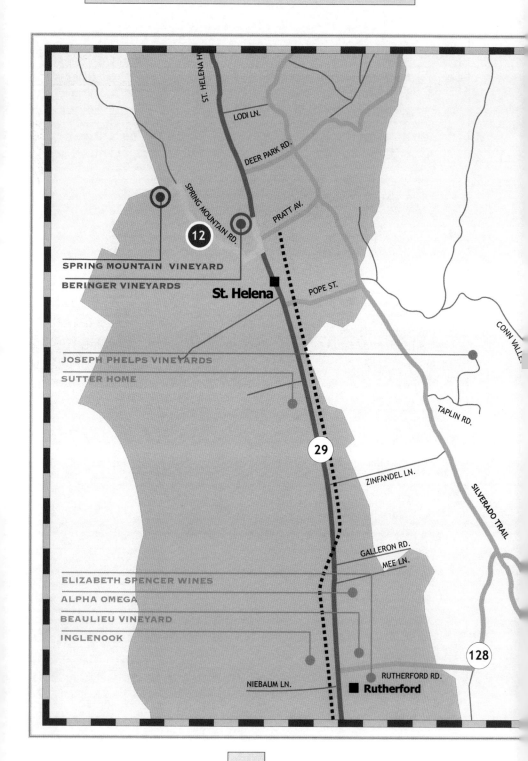

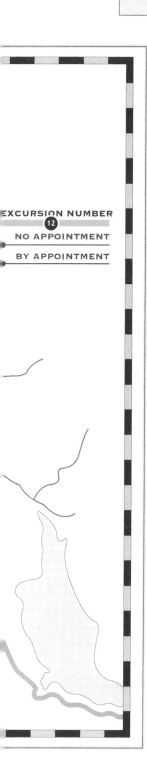

EXCURSION NUMBER
12
NO APPOINTMENT
BY APPOINTMENT

12

SPRING MT. TO BERINGER

Mansion to Mansion:

Both of these wineries' iconic mansions were designed by architect Albert Schroepfer: Villa Miravalle at Spring Mountain and the Rhine House Mansion at Beringer.

Spring Mountain Vineyard: Arrive at 2 pm for the 45-60 minute standing Classic Tasting. It is ideal for those who have limited time or just want a sampling of current releases. Arrive a little earlier at 1 pm for one of their more in-depth and highly recommended tours and tastings. The *Estate Tasting* and the *Library Vertical Tasting* last about 90-120 minutes. Both include a tour of the vineyard, winery and caves plus a seated tasting. Reservations are required. The grounds are beautiful, the staff are friendly and the wines are good.

Beringer Vineyards: Arrive here shortly after 3 pm and you should have plenty of time to take either of the tours that are offered. Beringer welcomes drop-in visitors for tastings but recommends reservations for its tours. The *Introduction to Beringer* tour is open to guests of all ages, takes 30 minutes and includes a visit to the Old Stone Winery and its wine-aging tunnels. The tour is given almost every half hour throughout the day. Offered three times a day at 10:30 am, 1:00 pm and 3:30 pm, is the one hour *Taste of Beringer* which includes a more extensive winery tour plus a tasting of four wines. If you'd rather only do a tasting, a sampling of three wines is available on the porch or at the tasting bar in the Rhine House Mansion. A flight of three lighter bodied wines is offered in the Old Winery Tasting Room.

Spring Mountain Vineyard

Spring Mountain Vineyard was established in 1968 by Michael Robbins. Unfortunately, the winery became better known as the setting for the television series Falcon Crest than it did for the quality of its wines. It was acquired in 1992 by Swiss financier Jacqui (Jacob) Eli Safra who then purchased several surrounding vineyards, restored its landmark Victorian buildings and badly tended vineyard, expanded on existing caves and constructed new ones for aging. The quality of the wines and reputation of the winery have since been dramatically restored. It is known for its Sauvignon Blanc, Cabernet Sauvignon and Bordeaux blends, *Elivette* and *Reserve*. Pinot Noir and Syrah are also produced. In 2010 Decanter Magazine World Wine Awards honored the 2005 Spring Mountain Vineyard Elivette with a Gold Medal.

This winery encompasses nearly a quarter of the vineyards under cultivation in the Spring Mountain appellation. According to consulting winemaker, Jac Cole, "when you taste a wine from this estate, you taste the essence of the appellation, the characteristics that define their wines and those of their neighbors."

SPRING MOUNTAIN VINEYARD	
WEBSITE:	www.springmountainvineyard.com
TASTING:	$$/4 tastes Classic Tasting
APPOINTMENT:	Required (arrange 24 hr. in advance)
ADDRESS:	2805 Spring Mountain Road,
	St. Helena, CA 94574
PHONE:	1+(877) 769-4637 or (707) 967-4188
HOURS:	Daily, 10:00 am - 4:00 pm
TOURS:	$$$$/Estate, $$$$/Library, $$$$/Elivette

Beringer Vineyards

Beringer Vineyards was founded in 1876 by German winemakers, Frederick and Jacob Beringer. The following year saw the construction of their winery and, later, tunnels for storage. In 1883 Frederick began construction of a 17-room mansion that was to be a re-creation of the Beringer family home on the Rhine River in Germany. Today the "Rhine House" is the iconic center of Beringer Vineyards where guests can enjoy Reserve or Library wine tastings or simply a glass of wine on the porch overlooking the grounds. Visitors can still see the tunnel of elm trees along the road in front of the winery that the brothers first planted in 1885. Designated a Historic District on the National Register of Historic Places, Beringer is the oldest continuously operating winery in the Napa Valley.

Several options for tours and tastings are available: check the website for details. Drop-ins for tastings in the Old Winery Tasting Room or for the Reserve and Limited Production tastings in the Reserve Tasting Bar at the historic Rhine House Mansion are welcomed.

BERINGER VINEYARDS	
WEBSITE:	www.beringer.com
TASTING:	$$/3 tastes Old Winery Room, $$/3 tastes Reserve Tasting
APPOINTMENT:	Not Required (recommended for tours)
ADDRESS:	2000 Main St.,
	St. Helena, CA 94574
PHONE:	1+(866) 708-9463 or (707) 963-8989 or (707) 967-4412
HOURS:	10 am - 6 pm (5/29 -10/22) & 10 am - 5 pm (10/23 - 5/28)
TOURS:	$$/Introduction to Beringer, $$$/Taste of Beringer

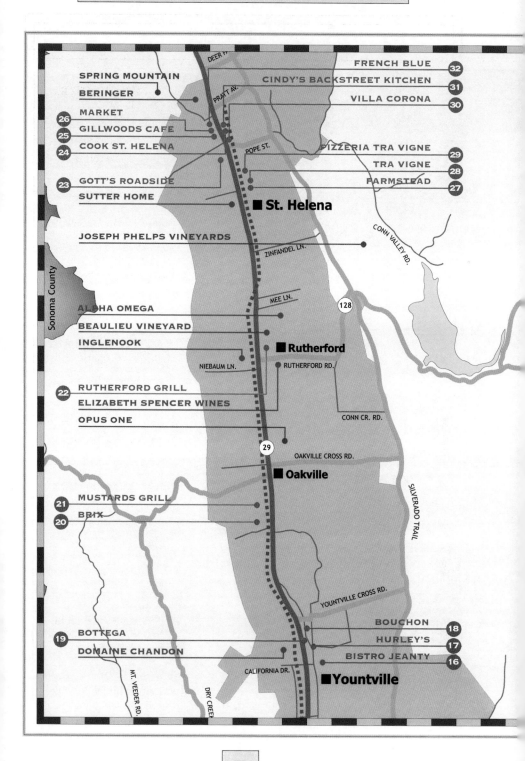

RESTAURANTS:
MID
NAPA
VALLEY

Restaurant Ratings

KEY:

RESTAURANTS ⓧⓧ

OVERALL QUALITY		COST PER PERSON	
		Under $10.............................($)	
Good:	★★★☆☆	$10 - $30..............................($$)	
Superior:	★★★★☆	$31 - $60..............................($$$)	
Exceptional:	★★★★★	Above $60.............................($$$$)	

MID NAPA VALLEY RESTAURANTS

BISTRO JEANTY: *6510 Washington St., Yountville, CA 94599,*
rating: ★★★★☆   *(707) 944-0103*
hours: M - Sun, 11:30 am -10:30 pm   *price: ($$$)*
website: www.bistrojeanty.com
category: French

 16

HURLEY'S RESTAURANT & BAR: *6518 Washington St., Yountville, CA 94599*
rating: ★★★⯪☆   *(707) 944-2345*
hours: Sun - Thu, 11:30 am –11 pm; Fri - Sat, 11:30 am –12 am   *price: ($$)*
website: www.hurleysrestaurant.com
category: New American

17

BOUCHON: *6534 Washington St., Yountville, CA 94599*
rating: ★★★★☆   *(707) 944-8037*
hours: M - F, 11:30 am -12 am   *price: ($$$)*
      Sat - Sun, 11am - 12 am
website: www.bouchonbistro.com
category: French

18

BOTTEGA RISTORANTE: *6525 Washington St., Yountville, CA 94599*
rating: ★★★★☆   *(707) 945-1050*
hours: Sun - Th, 5 pm - 9:30 pm & F - Sat, 5 pm - 10 pm (dinner)   *price: ($$$)*
      Th - Sun, 11:30 am - 2:30 pm (lunch)
website: www.botteganapavalley.com
category: Italian

19

BRIX: *7377 Saint Helena Hwy., Napa, CA 94558*
rating: ★★★★☆   *(707) 944-2749*
hours: M - Sat, 11:30 am - 9 pm   *price: ($$$)*
      Sun, 10 am - 9 pm
website: www.brix.com
category: New American

20

MID NAPA VALLEY RESTAURANTS

MUSTARDS GRILL: *7399 St. Helena Hwy, Yountville, CA 94558*
rating: ★★★★☆   *(707) 944-2424*
hours: *M - Th, 11:30 am - 9 pm*   *F, 11:30 am - 10 pm*   price: **($$$)**
       Sat, 11 am - 10 pm   *Sun, 11 am - 9 pm*
website: *www.mustardsgrill.com*
category: *New American*   **21**

RUTHERFORD GRILL: *1180 Rutherford Rd., Rutherford, CA 94573*
rating: ★★★★⯪   *(707) 963-1792*
hours: *Sun - Th, 11:30 am - 9:30 pm*   price: **($$)**
       F - Sat, 11:30 am - 10:30 pm
website: *www.rutherfordgrill.com*
category: *New & Traditional American*   **22**

GOTT'S ROADSIDE: *933 Main St., St Helena, CA 94574*
rating: ★★★★☆   *(707) 963-3486*
hours: *Summer: 10:30 am - 10:00 pm*   price: **($$)**
       Winter: 10:30 am - 9:00 pm
website: *http://gotts.com*
category: *Burgers, Traditional American, Fast-Food*   **23**

COOK: *1310 Main St., St. Helena, CA 94574*
rating: ★★★★☆   *(707) 963-7088*
hours: *M - Sat, 11:30 am - 10 pm*   price: **($$)**
       Sun, 5 pm - 10 pm
website: *www.cooksthelena.com*
category: *New American*   **24**

GILLWOODS CAFE: *1313 Main St., St. Helena, CA 94574,*
rating: ★★★⯪☆   *(707) 963-1788*
hours: *Daily, 7 am - 3 pm*   price: **($$)**
website: *www.gillwoodscafe.com*
category: *Breakfast, Brunch*   **25**

MID NAPA VALLEY RESTAURANTS

MARKET: 1347 Main St., St. Helena CA 94574
rating: ★★★★☆   (707) 963-3799
hours: M - Th, 11:30 am - 9 pm   Sun, 10 am - 9 pm   price: **($$)**
     F - Sat, 11:30 am - 10 pm
website: www.marketsthelena.com/
category: Traditional American   **26**

LONG MEADOW RANCH & FARMSTEAD: 738 Main St., St. Helena, CA 94574
rating: ★★★★☆   (707) 963-4555
hours: Daily, 11:30 am -10 pm   price: **($$)**
website: www.longmeadowranch.com
category: Wineries, New American   **27**

TRA VIGNE: 1050 Charter Oak Ave., St. Helena, CA 94574
rating: ★★★★☆   (707) 963-4444
hours: Sun - Th, 11:30 am - 9 pm   price: **($$$)**
     F - Sat, 11:30 am - 9:30 pm
website: www. travignerestaurant.com
category: Italian   **28**

PIZZERIA TRA VIGNE: 1016 Main St., St. Helena, CA 94574
rating: ★★★★☆   (707) 967-9999
hours: Sun - Th, 11:30 am - 9 pm   price: **($$)**
     F - Sat, 11:30 am - 9:30 pm
website: www.travignerestaurant.com
category: Pizza   **29**

VILLA CORONA: 1138 Main St., St. Helena CA 94574
rating: ★★★★☆   (707) 963-7812
hours: M - Sat, 9 am - 9 pm   price: **($$)**
     Sun, closed
website: www.villacoronash.com
category: Mexican   **30**

MID NAPA VALLEY RESTAURANTS

CINDY'S BACKSTREET KITCHEN: *1327 Railroad Ave., St. Helena, CA 94574*
rating: ★★★★☆   (707) 963-1200
hours: *Sun - Th, 11:30 am - 9 pm*   price: **($$)**
     F - Sat, 11:30 am - 9:30 pm
website: *www.cindysbackstreetkitchen.com*
category: *New American*   **31**

FRENCH BLUE: *1429 Main St., St Helena, CA 94574*
rating: ★★★★☆   (707) 968-9200
hours: *(Winter) Wed - Sun, 8 am - 9 pm & Mon, 8 am - 2 pm*   price: **($$)**
    (non-Winter) Wed - Fri, 9 am - 10 pm & Sat - Sun, 8 am - 10 pm
website: *http://frenchbluenapa.com/*
category: *New American*   **32**

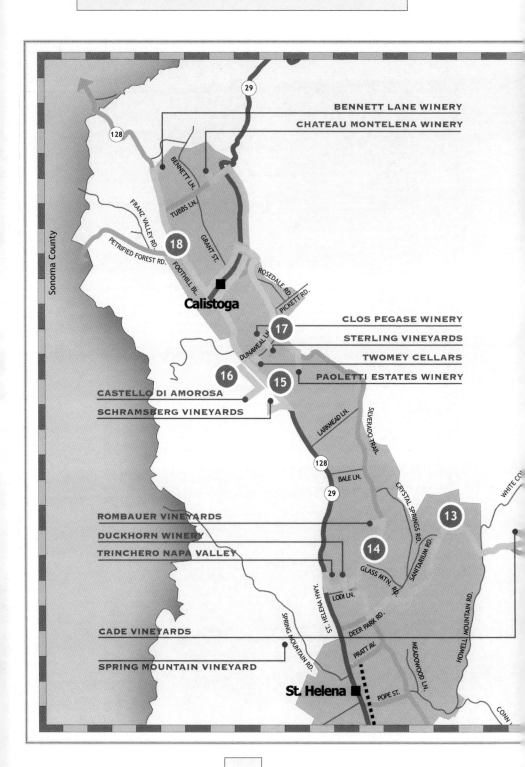

UPPER NAPA VALLEY:

Six Day-Trips to Twelve Upper Valley Wineries

From Duckhorn Winery to
Bennett Lane Winery

KEY:	Winery Guide	
Green: NO APPOINTMENT		Red: BY APPOINTMENT
COST PER PERSON		
Nominal.......(0 - $14)..........$		
Moderate.....($15 - $29).....$$		
Elevated.......($30 - $44).....$$$		
Spendy.........($45 PLUS).....$$$$		

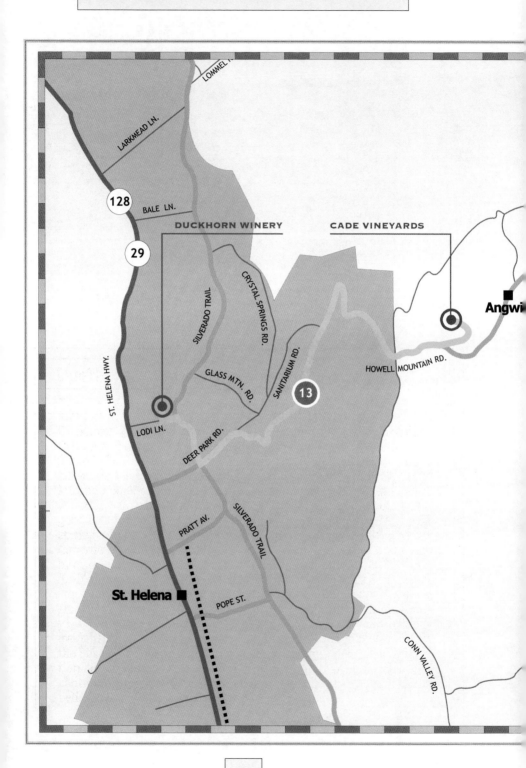

EXCURSION NUMBER
13
NO APPOINTMENT
BY APPOINTMENT

13

DUCKHORN TO CADE

From the Valley to the Mountain:

Duckhorn Winery: Weekend appointments are now required and weekday reservations are strongly suggested at Duckhorn Vineyards due to the current popularity of their tasting room. If your group is five or more, an appointment is required. The property is beautiful. The tasting room is situated in the charming Victorian-style Estate House which features a veranda around its side and back. Tastings are sit-down affairs at tables inside the tasting room, outside on the veranda or on the garden patio. Crackers and almonds are at your table for you to cleanse your palate. Your tastings come in separate glasses, each labeled with a souvenir identifying card. On weekends, for a nominal fee, you may order a cheese pairing to enjoy with your wine. A single level of tasting is offered: the Portfolio Tasting which showcases a selection of current release wines. The 90-minute *Estate Tour and Tasting* is by appointment.

Cade Vineyards: In no less beautiful a setting is Cade Winery. The tasting room and winery are located in the vineyard high atop Howell Mountain. The hour-long tasting is by appointment and usually only requires a call an hour in advance to arrange. Tastings of Cade's current wine releases are available either in the lounge-hospitality room or on the patio. The patio offers cushioned seating and an impressive infinity-pool water feature and both areas afford stunning views of the Napa Valley. A tour-and-cave tasting is also offered by appointment.

Duckhorn Vineyards

Duckhorn Vineyards specializes in Bordeaux varietals including Cabernet Sauvignon, Merlot and Sauvignon Blanc. It was co-founded by Dan and Margaret Duckhorn in 1976. Dan had acquired a taste for Merlot as a result of his travels through France's St. Émilion and Pomerol wine growing regions and while many Napa Valley wineries were using it as a blending grape, he thought it would be a good idea for his winery to focus on it as a stand-alone varietal. His strategy was a success and production grew from 1,600 cases of Cabernet Sauvignon and Merlot in 1978 to more than 20,000 cases by 2006. Over the last 30 years Duckhorn Vineyards has established itself as one of the premier Merlot producers in the Napa Valley.

Duckhorn Wine Company was created to oversee Duckhorn Vineyards and its various brands and operations. It oversees the Goldeneye label (Pinot Noir) of Anderson Valley, the Paraduxx Winery on the Silverado Trail and wines produced under the Decoy and Migration labels. In 2007 *GI Partners*, a private equity firm, purchased a controlling interest in the Duckhorn Wine Company for what is believed to have been in excess of $250 million.

DUCKHORN VINEYARDS	
WEBSITE:	*www.duckhorn.com*
TASTING:	*$$$/5 tastes Portfolio Tasting*
APPOINTMENT:	*Required for Estate Tour, for Sat & Sun tastings and for 5 or more*
ADDRESS:	*1000 Lodi Lane,*
	St. Helena, CA 94574
PHONE:	*1+(888) 354-8885 or (707) 963-7108*
HOURS:	*Daily, 10 am - 4 pm*
TOURS:	*$$$$/90-min. Estate Tour, 10:00 am, 12:00 pm & 2:30 pm*

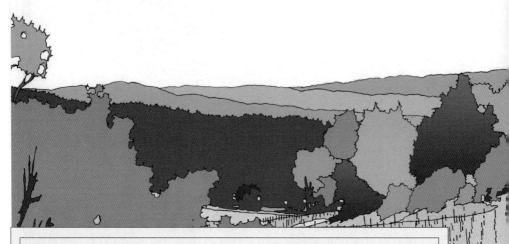

Cade Winery

Perched on a 54-acre Howell Mountain hillside at nearly 1,800 feet is Cade Winery, the latest addition to the 14-business enterprises owned or managed by the PlumpJack Group. PlumpJack was founded by former San Francisco Mayor Gavin Newsom and includes various restaurants, wineries (PlumpJack Winery, Oakville CA), stores, shops and resorts. Cade Winery is owned in partnership among Gavin Newsom, billionaire Gordon Getty and Cade General Manager John Conover. Opened in March 2009, the winery itself is a $16-million monument to environmentally sustainable winemaking. It is Napa Valley's first organically farmed winery to be awarded LEED Gold Certification by the U.S. Green Building Council.

Cade Winery produces four wines: Cade Estate Cabernet Sauvignon Howell Mountain, Cade Cabernet Sauvignon Howell Mountain (grapes sourced from local growers), *Cade Napa Cuvee Cabernet Sauvignon Napa Valley* (a Bordeaux-style blend) and Cade Sauvignon Blanc Napa Valley. To reduce the waste that results from "corked" wine, Cade is experimenting with screw-top closures.

CADE WINERY	
WEBSITE:	www.cadewinery.com
TASTING:	$$$/4 tastes
APPOINTMENT:	Required, by phone or online
ADDRESS:	360 Howell Mountain Rd. South,
	Angwin, CA 94508
PHONE:	(707) 965-2746
HOURS:	Daily, 10 am - 4 pm
TOURS:	$$$$/5 tastes Tour & Cave Tasting, 10 am, 1 pm, 3 pm

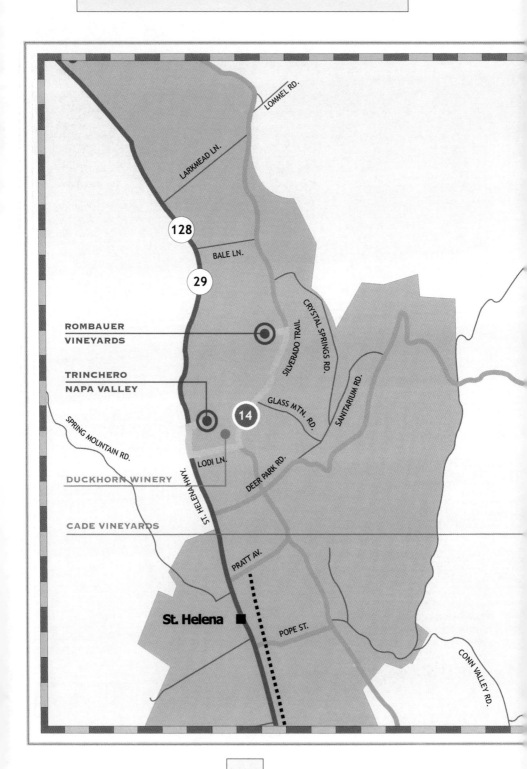

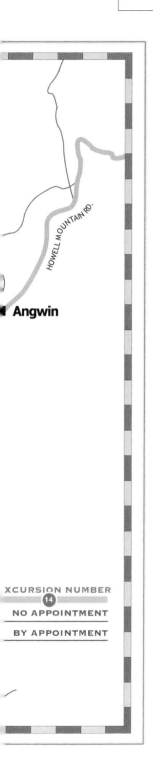

Angwin

XCURSION NUMBER
14
NO APPOINTMENT
BY APPOINTMENT

14

TRINCHERO TO ROMBAUER

From Fountains to Gardens:

Trinchero Napa Valley: Trinchero Napa Valley is a relatively new winery having only opened in 2009. But the Trinchero (pronounced Trin-kero) family has been producing wine in the Napa Valley for over 60 years and this winery represents the jewel in that crown. Located just two miles north of St. Helena, the winery occupies the site of the former Folie à Deux facility and its tasting room is in a restored 90-year old farm house. Picnics are not discouraged and tables and benches with vineyard views are available. An L-shaped wine bar greets you as you enter the tasting room and, in back, a living room annex with armchairs and sofa provides an inviting and relaxed wine tasting experience. No tours are currently offered and no appointment is needed for tasting, however, reservations are required for wine seminars.

Rombauer Vineyards: Rombauer Vineyards is not well marked, so look for the American flag in the driveway. Wind your way up the hill to the tasting room. On busy days, complimentary valet parking keeps things moving along. Situated next to the tasting room is an impressive garden with whimsical sculptures and tables for picnicking. The setting is woodsy with views of the valley through the trees. The tasting room itself is relatively small with several bar areas for tasting. No appointment is needed for groups of six or less. So confident is Rombauer in the robustness of their white wine that tastings here begin with the reds and conclude with the whites. They are justifiably famous for their Chardonnays.

Trinchero Napa Valley

Mario and Mary Trinchero arrived in the Napa Valley from New York City in 1948. They, along with Mario's brother John, purchased Sutter Home, refurbished it and commenced operations as a small mom and pop winery. In 1972 Mario's son Bob created the world's first White Zinfandel which went on to become an enormous success for Sutter Home and the Trinchero family. The family undertook a program of purchasing more than 220 acres in some of the most sought after appellations of the Napa Valley. In 2004 they purchased property north of St. Helena for Trinchero Napa Valley, a luxury winery honoring the legacy of Mario Trinchero, dedicated exclusively to Bordeaux grape varieties. By 2009 Trinchero Napa Valley produced its inaugural release of small production, estate grown, largely single-vineyard wines. The winery currently produces more than 12 different wines with a total production of only 12,000 cases annually. The Trinchero Napa Valley roster of wines includes Sauvignon Blanc, six Cabernet Sauvignons, two Merlots, Cabernet Franc, Petit Verdot and its Bordeaux blends, *Signature* and *Meritage*. Because production is limited, most of these wines are available only through the wine club or at the tasting room.

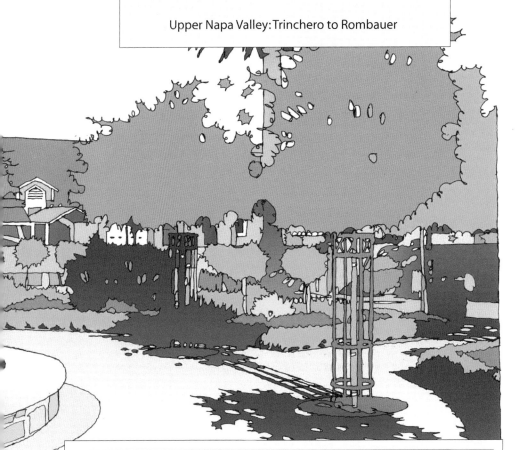

TRINCHERO NAPA VALLEY	
WEBSITE:	www.trincheronapavalley.com
TASTING:	**$$**/4 tastes Taste of Napa, **$$$**/3 tastes Legacy Flight
APPOINTMENT:	Not Required
ADDRESS:	3070 N. St. Helena Hwy.,
	St. Helena, CA 94574
PHONE:	1+(800) 473-4454 or (707) 963-1160
HOURS:	Daily, 10 am - 5 pm
TOURS:	No tours (See website for wine seminars by appointment.)

Rombauer Vineyards

Rombauer Vineyards sits atop a tree-covered hill overlooking the Napa Valley. It was founded in 1982 by Koerner and Joan Rombauer. Food and wine are important to the Rombauers. Koerner is the great nephew of Irma Rombauer, author of the "Joy of Cooking" which has been a staple of American kitchens since 1931. Koerner's family roots include a tradition of winemaking in the Rheingau region of Germany. He and Joan moved to the Napa Valley in the early 1970's in order to raise their children amidst the tranquility of an agricultural setting. They were soon attracted to winemaking and became partners in Conn Creek Winery. By 1980 the Rombauers had begun making wine under their own label at a neighbor's custom crush facility. The following year they sold their interest in Conn Creek and undertook construction of their own winery. Today Rombauer produces about 60,000 cases of wine a year, most of which is its very popular Carneros Chardonnay. It also produces Merlot, Zinfandel and Cabernet Sauvignon. Available only at the winery is a proprietary red Bordeaux blend called *Le Meilleur du Chai*. A late-harvest Chardonnay dessert wine called Joy and a port made from Zinfandel are also available.

ROMBAUER VINEYARDS	
WEBSITE:	*www.rombauer.com*
TASTING:	*$$/4 tastes Current Release, $$$/4 tastes Proprietor Flight*
APPOINTMENT:	*Recommended for 7 or more*
ADDRESS:	*3522 Silverado Trail North,*
	St. Helena, CA 94574
PHONE:	*1+(800) 622-2206 or (707) 963-5170*
HOURS:	*Daily, 10 am - 5 pm. Check website for holiday closures.*
TOURS:	*No tours offered. Picnics welcome.*

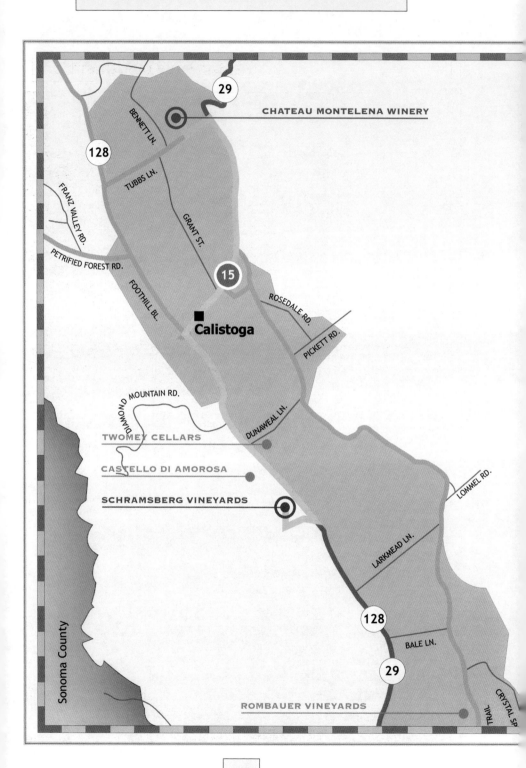

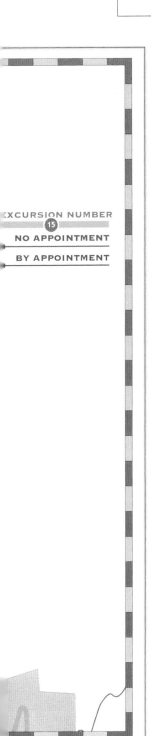

EXCURSION NUMBER

15

NO APPOINTMENT

BY APPOINTMENT

15
SCHRAMSBERG TO MONTELENA

From Cave to Chateau:

Schramsberg Vineyards: The Schramsberg Vineyards winery is at the end of a three mile road that meanders into the hills off Highway 29. Tours are by appointment and run about an hour and fifteen minutes. They are scheduled relatively often throughout the morning and afternoon. Consider first having lunch and then come for the 1:30 pm tour. You will be given a history of the winery, a tour of the caves and a wine tasting comprised of a flight of four sparkling wines and, on occasion, a bonus wine. Tour groups are relatively small: usually about 10 to 12 guests. The tours are both informative and entertaining and are highly recommended.

Chateau Montelena Winery: Chateau Montelena offers, in addition to a very popular *Vineyard Tour*, something called *Beyond Paris and Hollywood*. It recounts the 1976 Paris Tasting and the 2008 movie which popularized the event that helped secure the reputation of Napa Valley wines as world class. It is only available on Thursdays at 9:45 am. Reservations are required. The tour provides interesting facts and behind-the-scenes stories while you taste the Chardonnay that made it all possible. If you want to take either this tour or the *Vineyard Tour*, you should arrange to spend the morning at Chateau Montelena, have lunch, then continue on to Schramsberg. If, on the other hand, you're fine with just a tasting, do Schramsberg first then finish the day at Chateau Montelena with a four to five-wine sampling of their current releases.

Schramsberg Vineyards

Jacob Schram immigrated from Germany and eventually settled in the Napa Valley. He started Schramsberg Vineyards in 1862 and in 1870 he hired Chinese laborers to build underground aging cellars. He had shipbuilders construct a Victorian mansion in 1875 which, to this day, serves as the winery's iconic focal point. In 1965, fifty years after it had succumbed to the ravages of phylloxera and Prohibition, Jack and Jamie Davies purchased Schramsberg with the goal of producing fine California sparkling wine. Their 1965 Blanc de Blancs marked the first commercial use of Chardonnay in an American sparkling wine. In 1967 they followed it with their inaugural vintage of Blanc de Noirs made with Pinot Noir. Today, Hugh Davies carries on his parents' innovative tradition of winemaking.

Visits to Schramsberg are by appointment, take about an hour and fifteen minutes and usually include a sampling of four sparkling wines. Occasionally new tasting room experiences may be added so be sure to check their website for the latest information.

SCHRAMSBERG VINEYARDS	
WEBSITE:	www.schramsberg.com
TASTING:	$$$$/4 tastes & cave tour
APPOINTMENT:	Required
ADDRESS:	1400 Schramsberg Road,
	Calistoga, CA 94515
PHONE:	1+(800) 877-3623 or (707) 942-4558 (tour reservations)
HOURS:	Daily, 10 am - 4 pm
TOURS:	10 am, 11:30 am, 12:30 pm, 1:30 pm and 2:30 pm

Chateau Montelena

Alfred L. Tubbs bought 254 acres north of Calistoga in 1882 to grow grapes. By 1896 he had developed Chateau Montelena into the seventh largest winery in the Napa Valley. Winemaking came to an end with Prohibition and in 1958 the winery passed into the hands of Yort and Jeanie Frank. The real renaissance of Chateau Montelena, however, came later in 1972 under the leadership of Jim Barrett who had the vineyards replanted, the winery refitted with modern equipment and began once again producing wine.

In 1976 Chateau Montelena helped secure the reputation of California wines as world class. It was invited to participate in a blind tasting held at the Intercontinental Hotel in Paris in which four white Burgundies were pitted against six California Chardonnays. The nine French judges assumed the winning wine was one of their own but it turned out to be Chateau Montelena's 1973 Chardonnay. The outcome was seen as recognition that the California wine industry had finally come of age. Randall Miller's 2008 movie *Bottle Shock*, filmed in part at Chateau Montelena, is a retelling of this remarkable story.

CHATEAU MONTELENA	
WEBSITE:	www.montelena.com
TASTING:	*$$/4-5 tastes Current Release Tasting*
APPOINTMENT:	*Required for some tours & tastings*
ADDRESS:	*1429 Tubbs Lane,*
	Calistoga, CA 94515
PHONE:	*1+(800) 222-7288 or (707) 942-5105*
HOURS:	*Daily, 9:30 am - 4 pm*
TOURS:	*$$$/Vineyard (no appt.), $$$/Paris-Hollywood (by appt.)*

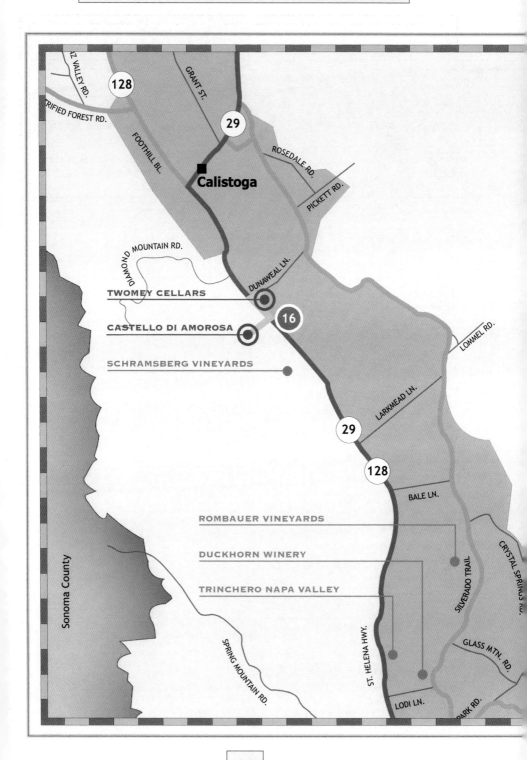

EXCURSION NUMBER
16
NO APPOINTMENT
BY APPOINTMENT

16

CASTELLO TO TWOMEY

From Over-the-Top to Understated:

Castello di Amorosa: Castello di Amorosa is an amazing addition to Napa Valley's landscape of winery experiences. Its entertainment value is off the chart. It is, after all, a full fledged 13th century Tuscan castle. For a moderate charge you may purchase the basic tasting which includes self-guided access to a limited portion of the castle. Instead, bite the bullet and choose the *Standard Tour and Tasting* (given every half-hour and lasting about an hour and three-quarters) for a guided tour of the whole castle plus a five-wine Premium Wine tasting. While well worth it, it's probably something you're only going to do once.

Twomey Cellars: Twomey Cellars (pronounced Two-me) is a relatively small 10,000 case winery whose tours must be set up in advance. They are usually offered twice a day and may be arranged by calling (707) 942-7026 or by emailing, *tours@twomeycellars.com*. Since you'll be coming from Castello di Amorosa, you'll probably not be in the mood for a tour anyway. So just relax and finish off the day with a tasting. Drop into their intimate tasting room and, for a nominal fee, enjoy a sampling of four of their offerings. The staff are friendly, helpful and informative and the grounds are attractive but, unlike Castillo di Amorosa, your visit to Twomey will be primarily for the wine. Although Twomey Cellars Calistoga is devoted to Merlot, they also specialize in Pinot Noir and Sauvignon Blanc which are also offered for tasting.

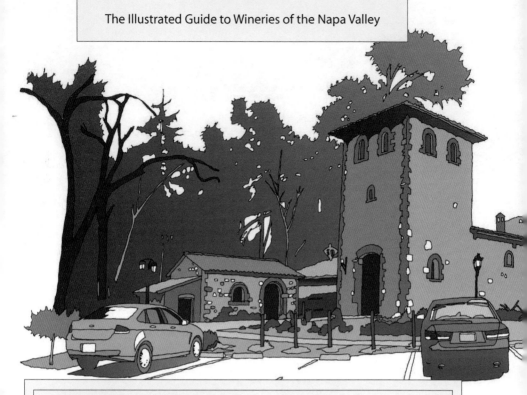

Castello di Amorosa

Castello di Amorosa is a full fledged multi-million dollar, 107 room re-creation of a 13th century Tuscan style castle. It is also a fully functioning working winery.

The temptation might be to dismiss this as some sort of Las Vegas themed gimmick designed simply to bring in the tourists. That this is an "attraction" is undeniable. But it is executed with sincerity, with attention to detail and authenticity. Daryl Sattui is the castle enthusiast and creator of Castello di Amorosa (Castle of Love) as well as the owner of V. Sattui Winery in St. Helena. All things considered, his latest creation is well worth a visit.

There is an entry fee which includes basic tasting privileges and limited access to the castle. There are a variety of additional tour and tasting options offered. For example, a one-and-three-quarter hour guided tour of the castle and winery followed by a private tasting of five Premium Wines is available. Reservations for all tours are highly suggested. A carriage tour of the vineyards plus a tasting is also available by appointment.

CASTELLO DI AMOROSA	
WEBSITE:	www.castellodiamorosa.com
TASTING:	**$$**/5 tastes Basic, **$$**/6 tastes Upgraded Reserve Tasting
APPOINTMENT:	Suggested for tours, required for 12 or more
ADDRESS:	4045 N. St. Helena Highway,
	Calistoga, CA 94515
PHONE:	(707) 967-6272
HOURS:	Daily, 9:30 am - 6 pm (5 pm winter), (closed Christmas)
TOURS:	**$$$**/Standard Tour & Tasting (See website for options.)

Twomey Cellars Calistoga

Twomey Cellars combines old world wine-making techniques with new world innovations to make California Merlot in the style of wines made in the Pomerol and St. Émilion districts of France. The winery was created in 1999 by the Duncan family, the same people who co-founded Silver Oak Cellars. Their goal was to do for Merlot what Silver Oak did for Cabernet Sauvignon: "to make food-friendly wine that is deliciously drinkable upon release."

Twomey has a winery and vineyards in the Russian River Valley as well. Between them they produce Merlot, Pinot Noir and Sauvignon Blanc: the Merlot and Sauvignon Blanc come from vineyards in the Napa Valley and the Pinot comes from the Russian River Valley.

A centuries old winemaking technique used in making Twomey's Merlot is called *soutirage traditional*. It is a slow, labor-intensive method of decanting wine from one barrel to another without the disruptive effect of pumping. The goal is to "preserve aromatics" and to "evolve" or soften the tannins.

TWOMEY CELLARS CALISTOGA	
WEBSITE:	*www.twomeycellars.com*
TASTING:	*$/4 tastes*
APPOINTMENT:	*Required for tours and for groups of 8 or more*
ADDRESS:	*1183 Dunaweal Lane,*
	Calistoga, CA 94515
PHONE:	*1+(800) 505-4850 or (707) 942-7026*
HOURS:	*10 am - 5 pm (4 pm winter) (Mon - Sat) & 11 am - 5 pm (Sun)*
TOURS:	*$$/by appointment*

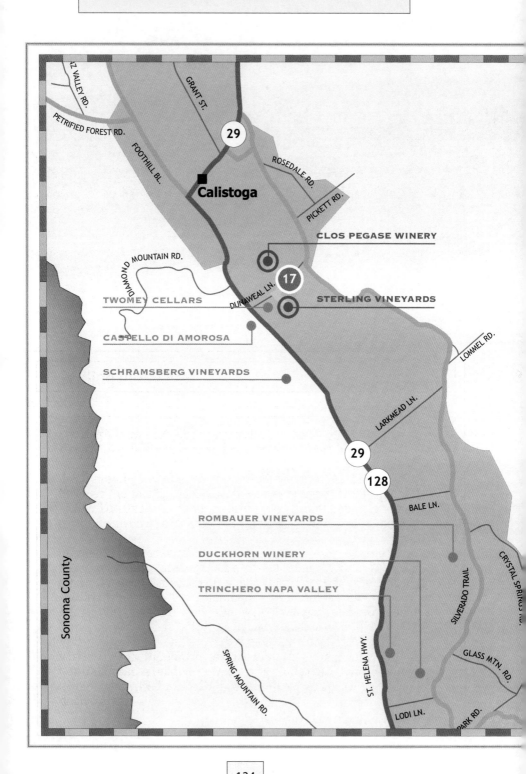

EXCURSION NUMBER
17
NO APPOINTMENT

BY APPOINTMENT

17

STERLING TO CLOS PEGASE

From Aerial to Art:

Sterling Vineyards: Arrive at Sterling Vineyards around noon. This has always been one of my favorite winery experiences. Enjoy the tranquil aerial tram ride up to the tasting room and the equally serene views of the valley below. The tram is moderately priced but be sure to check online for a discount coupon which is sometimes offered. The tour and tasting are both included in the price of the tram. The nice thing about Sterling is the self-guided tour: take it at your own pace, linger where you want and take in as much or as little as you like. You are greeted and given your first of five tastings as you make your way to the first overlook of crusher-destemmer machinery and steel-jacketed fermentation tanks. Pass by the barrel-aging rooms and receive your second tasting on the winery terrace with a vista of the entire Napa Valley to the south. Complete your tour and tasting seated in the tasting room, either inside or on the balcony, then exit by way of the gift shop where you may make your purchases.

Clos Pegase Winery: Located almost across the street is Clos Pegase Winery. Take in the world-class contemporary artwork as you make your way to and through the winery. Tours are given throughout the day, so if you've managed a couple of hours at Sterling and arrive at Clos Pegase around 3 pm you will be able to take advantage of the 60-minute tour. It covers both the winery and adjacent aging caves. There are two tiers of tastings currently offered: the Estate Tasting and the Reserve Tasting. Picnics are encouraged and a gift shop is available.

Sterling Vineyards

Sterling Vineyards' winery is perched on a hill 300 feet above the Napa Valley floor. It is modeled after the Greek island, Mykonos, where Sterling's founder, Peter Newton, once lived. Visitors reach the winery by aerial tram and are directed on a self-guided tour through the facility and onto the terrace overlooking the entire valley. The five-wine tastings are served throughout the tour and conclude inside the visitor center's tasting room.

Sterling produces six tiers of fine wine. The *Reserve* is the "richest most complete expression" of a varietal that they can make. The *Single Vineyard* focuses on wines that exemplify the terroir of specific vineyards e.g. Diamond Mountain Ranch and Three Palms Vineyard etc., while the *Napa Valley Appellation* concentrates on wines that reflect the characteristics of 14 diverse Napa Valley vineyards. *Cellar Club* wines are "non-core" or obscure varietals while the *Vintner's Collection* showcases wines from the Central Coast. A relative newcomer is *Made with Organic Grapes*, a line of wine produced of organically grown grapes from the Mendocino area.

STERLING VINEYARDS	
WEBSITE:	*www.sterlingvineyards.com*
TASTING:	*$$/5 tastes, tram & tour*
APPOINTMENT:	*Required for groups of 25 or more*
ADDRESS:	*1111 Dunaweal Lane,*
	Calistoga, CA 94515
PHONE:	*1+(800) 726-6136 or 1+(800) 206-7336 or (707) 942-3344*
HOURS:	*10:30 am - 4:30 pm (Mon - Fri) & 10 am - 5 pm (Sat - Sun)*
TOURS:	*Self-guided*

Clos Pegase Winery

The name, Clos Pegase, comes from the mythology of Pegasus, the winged horse, whose hooves brushed the earth as he flew into the sky. The earth opened for the "spring of the muses" to be released. That spring, it is said, watered the grapevines producing the wine that inspired the artists. Built in 1987, Clos Pegase Winery embodies the celebration of wine and art. "Clos", in French, means "enclosed vineyard", which in this case is the vineyard that surrounds the Michael Graves designed temple-to-wine-and-art winery. Almost 1,000 world-class works of art belonging to the owners, Jan Shrem and his late wife, Mitsuko, adorn the grounds.

The wines are "estate bottled" which means that the winery makes its wine from grapes grown solely from its own vine-yards. And the wine is completely produced, aged and bottled at the winery. They embrace "the idea of combining ancient winemaking practices with emerging technologies." Clos Pegase primarily makes five varietals: Cabernet Sauvignon, Merlot, Pinot Noir, Chardonnay and Sauvignon Blanc.

CLOS PEGASE WINERY	
WEBSITE:	www.clospegase.com
TASTING:	**$$**/4-5 tastes Estate Tasting, **$$$**/3 tastes Reserve Tasting
APPOINTMENT:	Required for 8 or more
ADDRESS:	1060 Dunaweal Lane,
	Calistoga, CA 94515
PHONE:	(707) 942-4981
HOURS:	Daily, 10:30 am - 5 pm (closed major holidays)
TOURS:	**$$$$**/5 tastes, "Connoisseur Tour & Tasting", daily by appointment

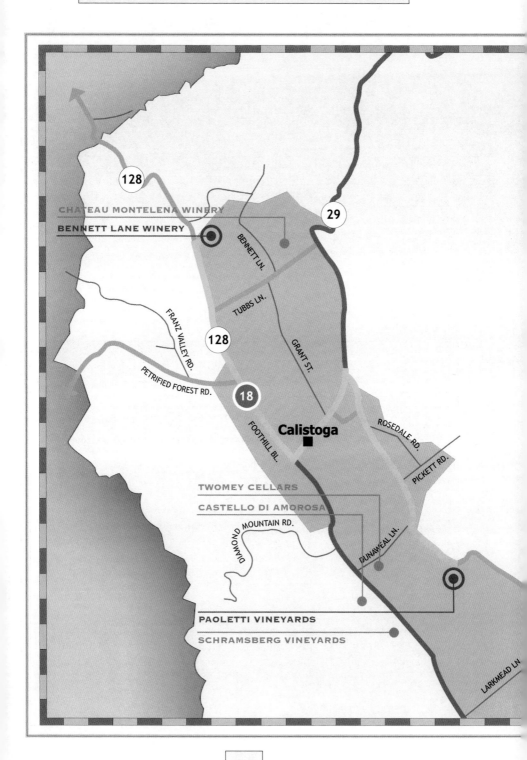

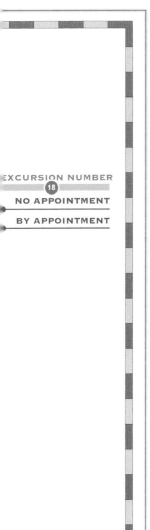

EXCURSION NUMBER
18
NO APPOINTMENT
BY APPOINTMENT

EL RD.

18

PAOLETTI TO BENNETT LANE

Cave Art to NASCAR:

Paoletti Vineyards: Paoletti Vineyards is a small winery with high quality and reasonably priced wines. Visits are by appointment Friday, Saturday and Sundays only. The moderately priced tasting includes six wines and a tour of the caves. Older vintages are sometimes available for tasting along with snacks of cheese, crackers and salami. The caves house barrels of wine and objects of art collected by the owners, Gianni and Lilia Paoletti. If you'd like to pack a lunch, there is a pleasant picnic area with patio tables, a waterfall fountain and an expansive view overlooking the pond and vineyards for your enjoyment.

Bennett Lane Winery: Although Bennett Lane Winery is open daily, remember to coordinate your appointment with Paoletti Vineyards' Friday-through-Sunday limited visiting hours. Bennett Lane's private tours can last from thirty minutes to an hour and may be arranged from just one hour to a day in advance. A tasting is offered with the tour and includes either a flight of four wines for a moderate fee or a flight of three Cabernets for slightly more. Food pairings, wine tasting classes and blending tutorials are also offered. Picnics are welcome and there is a courtyard off to one side of the tasting room where you may also enjoy your wine. Wines include Chardonnay, Cabernet Sauvignon and their *Maximus* blends. Bennett Lane is unique in that it is a NASCAR sponsor and you are invited to sit in one of their racing cars which can usually be found parked behind the winery.

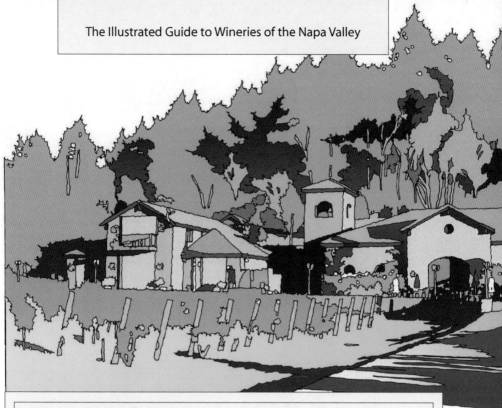

Paoletti Estates Winery

Gianni Paoletti was born in Venice and began cooking when he was seventeen. In 1964 he came to Los Angeles where he worked in a succession of restaurants and eventually opened his own in Brentwood which he named Peppone. Whenever he is in Los Angeles he can still be found working long hours in his restaurant. Paoletti's interest in wine harkens back to his days of pairing wine with food in cooking school and his restaurant currently boasts a wine list of more than 1,200 selections. In the 1970's he began making trips to the Napa Valley where he gradually acquired vineyard property including the property which today houses his winery and personal home. Paoletti Estates Winery remains small and produces only 3,500 cases annually. It is a state-of-the-art facility with modern equipment and an extensive cave system housing wine and a collection of stained glass and sculpture. Gianni's wife Lilia is the operational and administrative manager. Paoletti takes pride in offering wine that is priced for far less than many comparable wines produced in the Napa Valley. The winery specializes in Bordeaux and Super Tuscan blends. If it's available for tasting, be sure to try their highly rated Non-Plus Ultra Napa Valley Red Wine.

PAOLETTI ESTATES WINERY	
WEBSITE:	www.paolettivineyards.com
TASTING:	**$$**/6 tastes & cave tour
APPOINTMENT:	Required
ADDRESS:	4501 Silverado Trail,
	Calistoga, CA 94515
PHONE:	(707) 942-0689
HOURS:	11 am - 5 pm (Fri - Sat), 11 am - 4 pm (Sun)
TOURS:	By appointment (tour included with tasting)

Bennett Lane Winery

Opened in fall of 2003 by Randy and Lisa Lynch, Bennett Lane is already well known for its Cabernet Sauvignon and *Maximus*, a proprietary blend of Cabernet, Merlot and Syrah. Partner to *Maximus* is their *White Maximus,* "an aromatic blend of Sauvignon Blanc, Chardonnay and Muscat." The winery produces about 11,000 cases of wine annually, all from Napa Valley grapes. The grapes are sourced from several vineyards in the valley including 22.5 acres adjacent to the winery itself. The owners' goal is to make good wine at a reasonable price. The tasting room has a stand-up bar and a courtyard-patio with tables outside. Picnics are welcomed.

Bennett Lane Winery, in part, represents an effort to specifically target race car fans as a market for premium wine. In his youth, Randy was a race car driver and today both he and Lisa continue to be race car enthusiasts. Theirs is the first winery to own and sponsor a NASCAR racing team. Before purchasing Bennett Lane, Randy founded a successful marketing firm, the RW Lynch Company, in San Ramon, California.

BENNETT LANE WINERY	
WEBSITE:	www.bennettlane.com
TASTING:	**$$**/4 tastes Overview, **$$$**/3 tastes Reserve
APPOINTMENT:	Required 1 hr. in advance weekdays, 24 hrs. weekends
ADDRESS:	3340 Hwy 128,
	Calistoga, CA 94515
PHONE:	1+(877) 629-6272 or (707) 942-6684
HOURS:	Daily, 10 am - 5:30 pm
TOURS:	Quick tour included with tasting as time permits

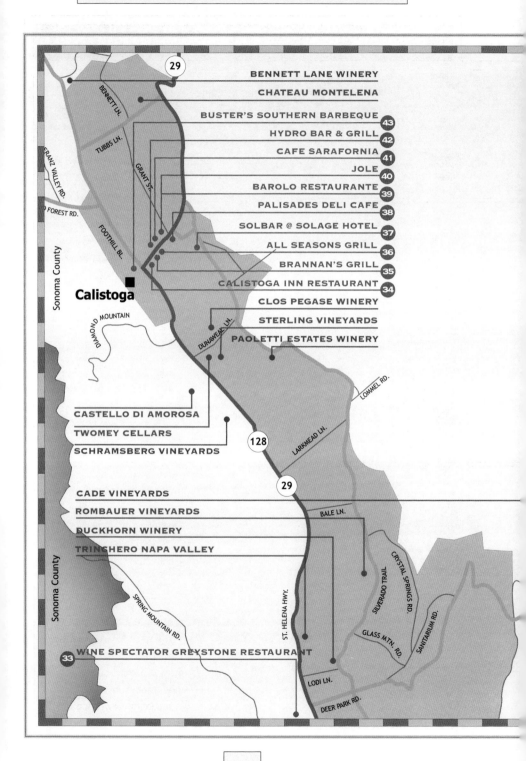

BENNETT LANE WINERY

CHATEAU MONTELENA

BUSTER'S SOUTHERN BARBEQUE 43

HYDRO BAR & GRILL 42

CAFE SARAFORNIA 41

JOLE 40

BAROLO RESTAURANTE 39

PALISADES DELI CAFE 38

SOLBAR @ SOLAGE HOTEL 37

ALL SEASONS GRILL 36

BRANNAN'S GRILL 35

CALISTOGA INN RESTAURANT 34

CLOS PEGASE WINERY

STERLING VINEYARDS

PAOLETTI ESTATES WINERY

CASTELLO DI AMOROSA

TWOMEY CELLARS

SCHRAMSBERG VINEYARDS

CADE VINEYARDS

ROMBAUER VINEYARDS

DUCKHORN WINERY

TRINCHERO NAPA VALLEY

33 WINE SPECTATOR GREYSTONE RESTAURANT

Calistoga

Sonoma County

BENNETT LN.

TUBBS LN.

GRANT ST.

FOOTHILL BL.

FRANZ VALLEY RD.

FOREST RD.

DIAMOND MOUNTAIN

DUNAWEAL LN.

LOMMEL RD.

LARKMEAD LN.

BALE LN.

SPRING MOUNTAIN RD.

ST. HELENA HWY.

SILVERADO TRAIL

CRYSTAL SPRINGS RD.

GLASS MTN. RD.

SANITARIUM RD.

LODI LN.

DEER PARK RD.

29

128

29

RESTAURANTS:
UPPER
NAPA
VALLEY

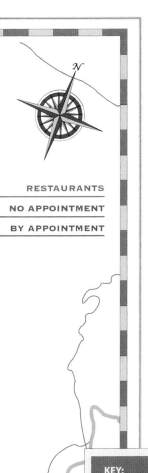

RESTAURANTS
NO APPOINTMENT
BY APPOINTMENT

Angwin

KEY:	Restaurant Ratings		
		RESTAURANTS XX	
OVERALL QUALITY		**COST PER PERSON**	
		Under $10............................(*$*)	
Good:	★★★☆☆	$10 - $30.............................(*$$*)	
Superior:	★★★★☆	$31 - $60.............................(*$$$*)	
Exceptional:	★★★★★	Above $60............................(*$$$$*)	

UPPER NAPA VALLEY RESTAURANTS

WINE SPECTATOR GREYSTONE: 2555 Main St., St Helena, CA 94574

rating: ★★★★☆   (707) 967-1010

hours: Sun - Th, 11:30 am - 9 pm   F - Sat, 11:30 am - 9:30 pm   price: **($$$)**

     closed, Thanksgiving & Christmas

website: www.ciachef.edu/restaurants/wsgr/

category: Cooking School, New American

33

CALISTOGA INN RESTAURANT & BREWERY: 1250 Lincoln Ave., Calistoga, CA 94515

rating: ★★★⯪☆   (707) 942-4101

hours: Mon - Fri, 11:30 pm - 9:30 pm   price: **($$)**

     Sat - Sun, 11 am - 9:30 pm

website: www.calistogainn.com

category: Traditional American

34

BRANNAN'S GRILL: 1374 Lincoln Ave., Calistoga, CA 94515

rating: ★★★⯪☆   (707) 942-2233

hours: Sun - Th, 11:30 am - 9:30 pm   price: **($$$)**

     F - Sat, 11:30 am - 10:30 pm

website: www.brannansgrill.com

category: Traditional American

35

ALL SEASONS BISTRO: 1400 Lincoln Ave., Calistoga, CA 94515

rating: ★★★★☆   (707) 942-9111

hours: Tu - Sun, 12 pm - 2:30 pm (lunch)   price: **($$)**

     Tu - Sun, 5:30 pm - 9 pm (dinner)

website: www. allseasonsnapavalley.net

category: New American

36

SOLBAR @ THE SOLAGE HOTEL: 755 Silverado Trail, Calistoga, CA 94515

rating: ★★★★☆   (707) 226-0850

hours: Daily, 7 am - 11 pm   price: **($$$)**

     Sun, 11:30 am - 3 pm (brunch)

website: www.solbarnv.com/

category: New American

37

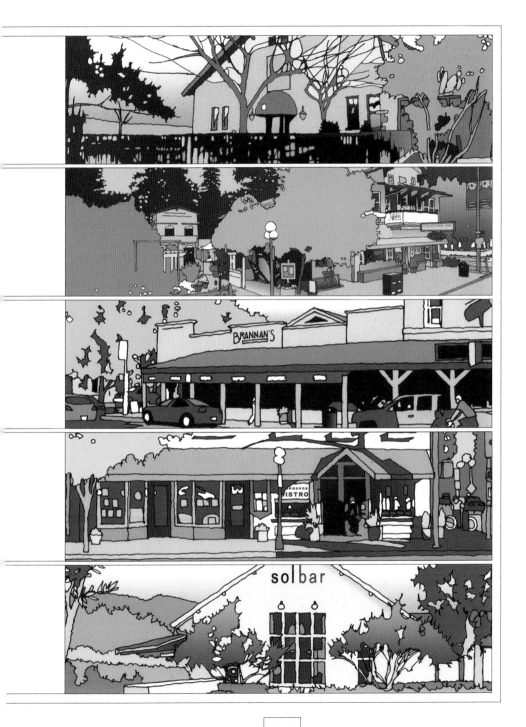

UPPER NAPA VALLEY RESTAURANTS

PALISADES DELI AND CAFE: 1458 Lincoln Ave., Calistoga, CA 94515

rating: ★★★★☆

hours: call for hours

website: www.palisadescafe.com

category: Deli

(707) 942-0145

price: **($)**

38

BAROLO: 1457 Lincoln Ave., Calistoga, CA 94515

rating: ★★★⯪☆

hours: Sun - Th, 4:30 pm - 9 pm

F - Sat, 4:30 pm - 9:30 pm

website: www.barolocalistoga.com

category: New American, Italian

(707) 942-9900

price: **($$)**

39

JoLe: 1457 Lincoln Ave., Calistoga, CA 94515

rating: ★★★★☆

hours: Sun - Th, 5 pm - 9 pm

F - Sat, 5 pm - 11 pm

website: www.jolerestaurant.com

category: New American

(707) 942-5938

price: **($$$)**

40

CAFE SARAFORNIA: 1413 Lincoln Ave., Calistoga, CA 94515

rating: ★★★⯪☆

hours: Daily, 7 am - 2:30 pm

breakfast all day & lunch starts at 11 am

website: www.cafesarafornia.com/

category: Breakfast, Traditional American

(707) 942-0555

price: **($)**

41

HYDRO BAR & GRILL: 1403 Lincoln Ave., Calistoga, CA 94515

rating: ★★★☆☆

hours: Daily, 8:30 am - 10 pm

website: none

category: Restaurant, Bar

(707) 942-9777

price: **($$)**

42

UPPER NAPA VALLEY RESTAURANTS

BUSTER'S SOUTHERN BBQ: *1207 Foothill Blvd., Calistoga CA*

rating: *(707) 942-5605*

hours: M - Sat, 9 am - 8 pm   *price:* **($)**
       Sun, 11 am - 6:30 pm

website: www. busterssouthernbbq.com

category: Barbecue

43

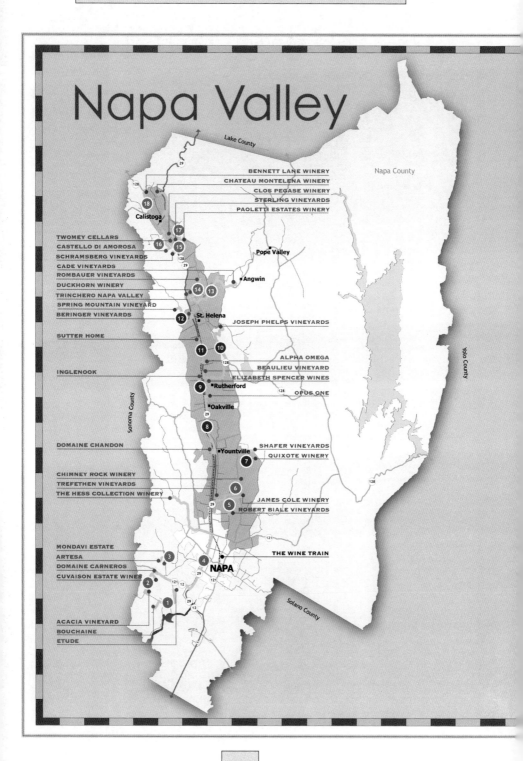

APPENDIX: A

Tours and Tastings:

Wineries *frequently* change how they schedule and what they charge for tastings and tours, so it is wise to check before visiting. You can use this guide to see how expensive one winery might be relative to another but other details will likely change over time. Call or check websites for the most current information.

EXCURSION NUMBER
XX
NO APPOINTMENT

BY APPOINTMENT

KEY:	Tour Schedules		
Green: NO APPOINTMENT		**Red: BY APPOINTMENT**	
TOUR DURATION TIMES		**COST PER PERSON**	
15 min:		Nominal...........(0 - $14)..........$	
30 min:		Moderate........($15 - $29).....$$	
60 min:		Elevated...........($30 - $44).....$$$	
90 min:		Spendy.............($45 PLUS).....$$$$	

Tour Schedules: 1. Etude to Bouchaine

(877) 586-9361	Etude	Daily	No general tour	(800) 654-9463	Bouchaine Vineyards	Daily	No general tour
	9				9		
	10				10		
	11				11		
	12				12		
	1				1		
	2				2		
	3				3		
	4				4		
	5				5		
	6				6		

Tour Schedules: 2. Acacia to Cuvaison

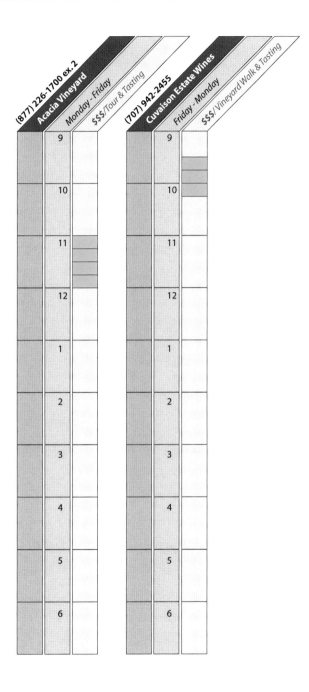

Tour Schedules: 3. Mondavi to Artesa

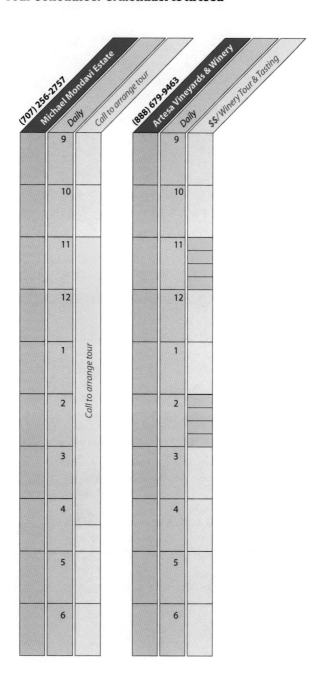

Tour Schedules: 4. Carneros to Hess

(800) 716-2788 — Domaine Carneros — Daily — $$$/Art of Sparkling Wine — additional Sat. tour (Jun - Oct)

(707) 255-1144 — Hess Collection — Daily — $/Complimentary Tour

Time	Domaine Carneros (Art of Sparkling Wine)	additional Sat. tour	Hess Collection (Complimentary Tour)
9			
10			▓
11	▓		▓
12	▓		▓
1	▓		▓
2	▓		▓
3	▓		▓
4	▓	▓	
5		▓	
6			

Tour Schedules: 5. Biale to Cole

(707) 257-7555	Robert Biale Vineyards	Daily	No general tours	(707) 251-9905	James Cole Estate Winery	Daily	No general tours
	9				9	
	10				10	
	11				11	
	12				12	
	1				1	
	2				2	
	3				3	
	4				4	
	5				5	
	6				6	

Tour Schedules: 6. Trefethen to Chimney Rock

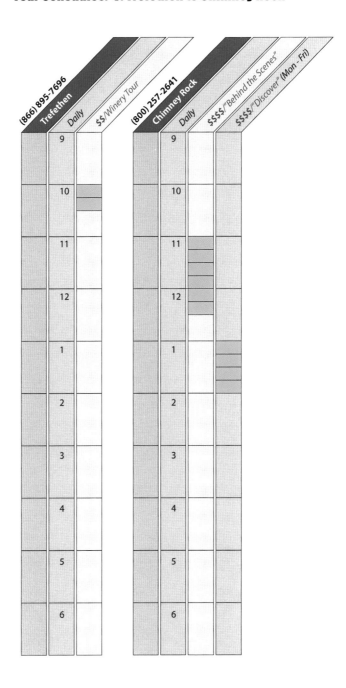

Tour Schedules: 7. Quixote to Shafer

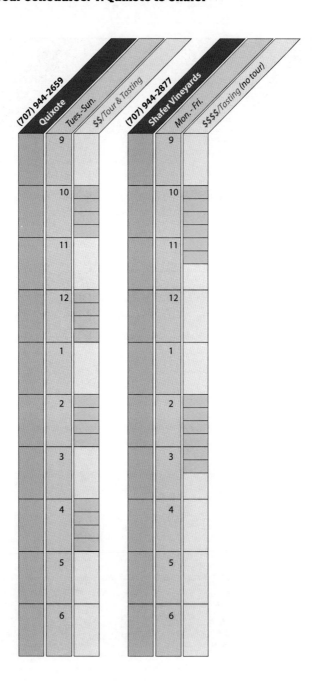

Tour Schedules: 8. Chandon to Opus

(888) 242-6366 Domaine Chandon	Daily	$$$/Rosé Tour & Tasting	$$$/Étoile Tour & Tasting	$$$/Vintage Tour & Tasting		(800) 292-6787 Opus One	Daily	$$$$/Estate Tour	$$$$/Double Vintage Tour
9						9			
10		▓				10			▓
11		▓				11			▓
12	▓					12			▓
1						1	▓		
2						2	▓	▓	
3			▓			3		▓	
4			▓			4			
5						5			
6						6			

Tour Schedules: 9. Spencer to Inglenook

(707) 963-4762 Elizabeth Spencer Wines	Daily	No general tour	(707) 968-1161 Inglenook	Daily	$$$$/ Inglenook Experience	Dec-July (F,Sat)/Aug-Nov (daily)	Dec-July (Sun-Th)	$$$$/Elevage May-Oct (F - Sun)
9				9				
10				10				
11				11				
12				12				
1				1				
2				2				
3				3				
4				4				
5				5				
6				6				

Tour Schedules: 10. Beaulieu to Phelps

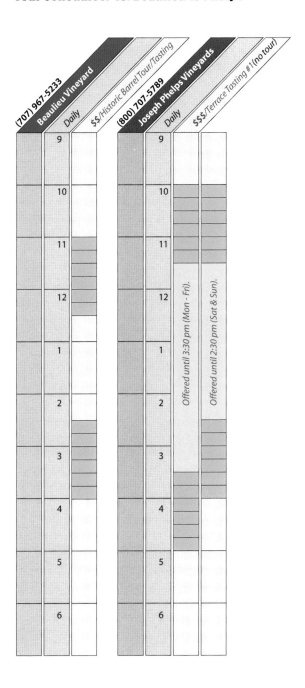

Tour Schedules: 11. Alpha Omega to Sutter Home

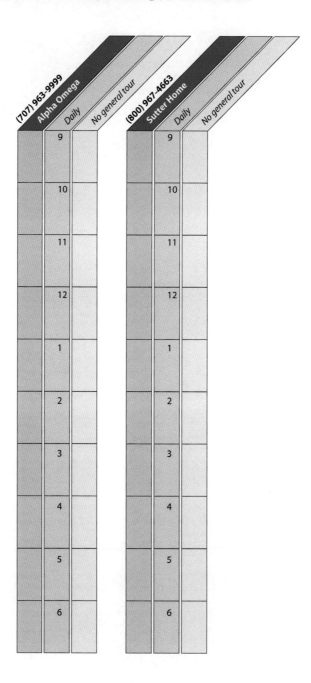

(707) 963-9999 Alpha Omega	Daily	No general tour	(800) 967-4663 Sutter Home	Daily	No general tour
	9			9	
	10			10	
	11			11	
	12			12	
	1			1	
	2			2	
	3			3	
	4			4	
	5			5	
	6			6	

Tour Schedules: 12. Spring Mt. to Beringer

Spring Mountain Vineyard — (707) 967-4188

Time	Daily	$$/Classic Tasting	$$$/Estate Tasting & Walk	$$$$/Library Vertical Tasting	$$$$/Explore Elivette Tasting
9					
10	Call to arrange (tasting only).				
11					
12					
1					
2					
3					
4					
5					
6					

Beringer Vineyards — (707) 963-8989

Time	Daily	$$/Introduction to Beringer	$$$/Taste of Beringer
9			
10			
11			
12			
1			
2			
3			
4			
5			
6			

Tour Schedules: 13. Duckhorn to Cade

(888) 354-8885	Duckhorn Vineyards	Daily	$$$$/Estate Tour & Tasting
	9		
	10		
	11		
	12		
	1		
	2		
	3		
	4		
	5		
	6		

(707) 965-2746	Cade Winery	Daily	$$$/Current Release Tasting	$$$$/Tour & Cave Tasting
	9	Offered nearly every hour on the hour until 3 pm.		
	10			
	11			
	12			
	1			
	2			
	3			
	4			
	5			
	6			

Tour Schedules: 14. Rombauer to Trinchero

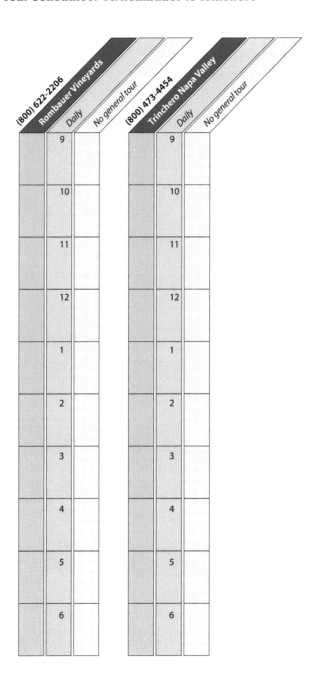

(800) 622-2206	Rombauer Vineyards	Daily	No general tour	(800) 473-4454	Trinchero Napa Valley	Daily	No general tour
		9				9	
		10				10	
		11				11	
		12				12	
		1				1	
		2				2	
		3				3	
		4				4	
		5				5	
		6				6	

Tour Schedules: 15. Schramsberg to Montelena

(707) 942-4558 — Schramsberg Vineyards — Daily — $$$$/Cave Tour & Tasting

(800) 222-7288 — Chateau Montelena — Thurs — $$$/Paris-Hollywood — Mon & Weds — $$$/Vineyard

9 10 11 12 1 2 3 4 5 6

Tour Schedules: 16. Castello to Twomey

(707) 967-6272	Castello de Amorosa	Daily	$$/Admission & Tasting	$$/Admission & Upgrade	$$$/Tour & Tasting	$$$/Upgraded Reserve Tour
	9		Limited self-guided tour & tasting.	Limited self-guided tour & reserve tasting.	Offered approximately every half-hour.	Offered approximately every half-hour.
	10					
	11					
	12					
	1					
	2					
	3					
	4					
	5					
	6					

(707) 942-7026	Twomey Cellars	Daily	$$/tour with tasting
	9		Call to arrange tour.
	10		
	11		
	12		
	1		
	2		
	3		
	4		
	5		
	6		

171

Tour Schedules: 17. Sterling to Clos Pegase

(800) 726-6136	Sterling Vineyards	Daily	$$/Self-Guided Tour & Tasting	(707) 942-4981	Clos Pegase Winery	Daily	$$$$/Connoisseur Tour/Tasting
	9				9		
	10				10		
	11				11		
	12				12		
	1		Self guided winery tour		1		
	2				2		
	3				3		
	4				4		
	5				5		
	6				6		

Tour Schedules: 18. Paoletti to Bennett

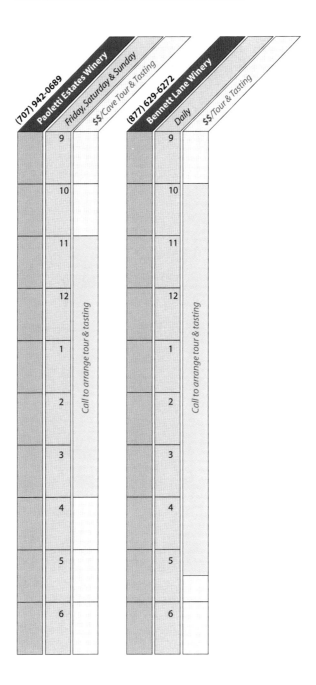

(707) 942-0689	Paoletti Estates Winery	Friday, Saturday & Sunday	$$/Cave Tour & Tasting	(877) 629-6272	Bennett Lane Winery	Daily	$$/Tour & Tasting
	9				9		
	10				10		
	11		Call to arrange tour & tasting		11		Call to arrange tour & tasting
	12				12		
	1				1		
	2				2		
	3				3		
	4				4		
	5				5		
	6				6		

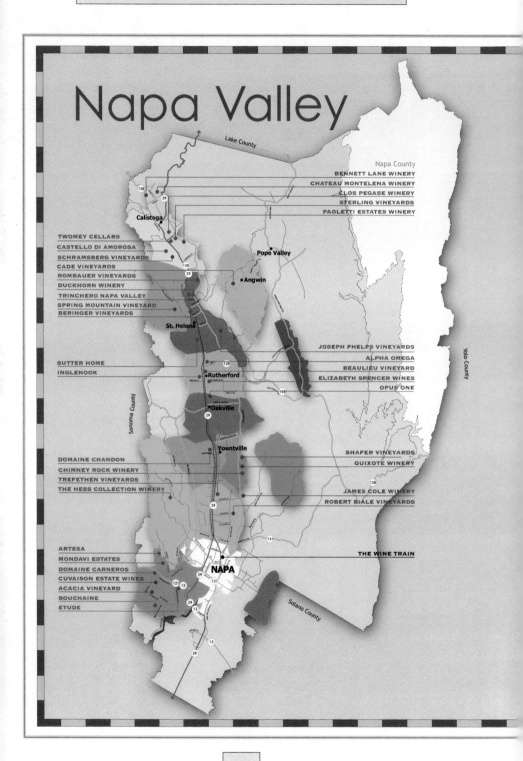

Napa Valley

Lake County

Napa County

BENNETT LANE WINERY
CHATEAU MONTELENA WINERY
CLOS PEGASE WINERY
STERLING VINEYARDS
PAOLETTI ESTATES WINERY

Calistoga

TWOMEY CELLARS
CASTELLO DI AMOROSA
SCHRAMSBERG VINEYARDS
CADE VINEYARDS
ROMBAUER VINEYARDS
DUCKHORN WINERY
TRINCHERO NAPA VALLEY
SPRING MOUNTAIN VINEYARD
BERINGER VINEYARDS

Pope Valley

Angwin

St. Helena

JOSEPH PHELPS VINEYARDS
ALPHA OMEGA
SUTTER HOME
INGLENOOK
BEAULIEU VINEYARD
Rutherford
ELIZABETH SPENCER WINES
OPUS ONE

Oakville

Yountville

Sonoma County

SHAFER VINEYARDS
QUIXOTE WINERY

DOMAINE CHANDON
CHIMNEY ROCK WINERY
TREFETHEN VINEYARDS
THE HESS COLLECTION WINERY
JAMES COLE WINERY
ROBERT BIALE VINEYARDS

Yolo County

ARTESA
MONDAVI ESTATES
THE WINE TRAIN
DOMAINE CARNEROS
CUVAISON ESTATE WINES
ACACIA VINEYARD
BOUCHAINE
ETUDE

NAPA

Solano County

NO APPOINTMENT

BY APPOINTMENT

APPENDIX: B

A Word About Appellations:

Grapes benefit from growth in locations and microclimates for which they are best suited. Vintners and growers give these areas names, or appellations, reflecting their regional designation. Grapes grown in these regions have specific and characteristic qualities which are unique to these areas.

The Napa Valley is itself a sub-appellation of the Napa County Appellation. There are 15 additional Napa Valley sub-appellations, or AVAs (American Viticultural Areas), as designated below. The Calistoga AVA is the most recent addition. A viticultural area is a subset of appellation. It's just one kind of appellation.

NAPA VALLEY VITICULTURAL AREAS		
		ATLAS PEAK AVA
		CALISTOGA AVA
		CARNEROS AVA
		CHILES VALLEY AVA
		DIAMOND MOUNTAIN AVA
		HOWELL MOUNTAIN AVA
		MOUNT VEEDER AVA
		OAK KNOLL AVA
		OAKVILLE AVA
		RUTHERFORD AVA
		ST. HELENA AVA
		SPRING MOUNTAIN AVA
		STAGS LEAK DISTRICT AVA
		WILD HORSE VALLEY AVA
		YOUNTVILLE AVA
		NAPA VALLEY AVA

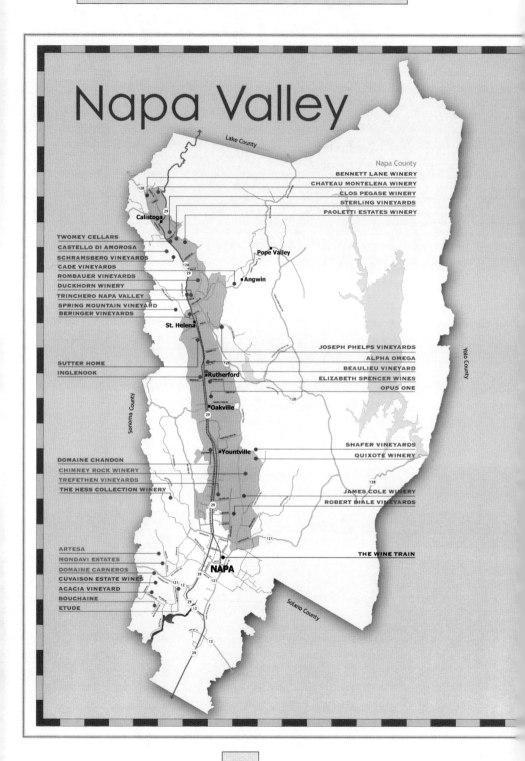

Napa Valley

Lake County

Napa County

BENNETT LANE WINERY
CHATEAU MONTELENA WINERY
CLOS PEGASE WINERY
STERLING VINEYARDS
PAOLETTI ESTATES WINERY

Calistoga

TWOMEY CELLARS
CASTELLO DI AMOROSA
SCHRAMSBERG VINEYARDS
CADE VINEYARDS
ROMBAUER VINEYARDS
DUCKHORN WINERY
TRINCHERO NAPA VALLEY
SPRING MOUNTAIN VINEYARD
BERINGER VINEYARDS

Pope Valley

Angwin

St. Helena

JOSEPH PHELPS VINEYARDS
ALPHA OMEGA
BEAULIEU VINEYARD
ELIZABETH SPENCER WINES
OPUS ONE

SUTTER HOME
INGLENOOK

Rutherford

Oakville

Sonoma County

Yolo County

SHAFER VINEYARDS
QUIXOTE WINERY

Yountville

DOMAINE CHANDON
CHIMNEY ROCK WINERY
TREFETHEN VINEYARDS
THE HESS COLLECTION WINERY

JAMES COLE WINERY
ROBERT BIALE VINEYARDS

ARTESA
MONDAVI ESTATES
DOMAINE CARNEROS
CUVAISON ESTATE WINES
ACACIA VINEYARD
BOUCHAINE
ETUDE

NAPA

THE WINE TRAIN

Solano County

APPENDIX: C

A List of Wineries Reviewed:

NO APPOINTMENT

BY APPOINTMENT

WINERIES REVIEWED BY LOCATION

LOWER NAPA VALLEY

MID NAPA VALLEY

MID NAPA VALLEY (continued)

72-73	OPUS ONE
66-67	QUIXOTE WINERY
64-65	SHAFER VINEYARDS
94-95	SPRING MOUNTAIN VINEYARD
90-91	SUTTER HOME

UPPER NAPA VALLEY

144-145	BENNETT LANE WINERY
114-115	CADE WINERY
130-131	CASTELLO DI AMOROSA
126-127	CHATEAU MONTELENA
138-139	CLOS PEGASE WINERY
112-113	DUCKHORN VINEYARDS
142-143	PAOLETTI ESTATES WINERY
120-121	ROMBAUER VINEYARDS
124-125	SCHRAMSBERG VINEYARDS
136-137	STERLING VINEYARDS
118-119	TRINCHERO NAPA VALLEY
132-133	TWOMEY CELLARS

ACKNOWLEDGMENTS

Many thanks to Jac and Ami Cole for their kind words and support. I'd also like to thank Jac for encouraging my interest in wine over the years and for the behind-the-scenes access and insights into some of the wineries and people in the industry. And a special thanks for his constructive input and particularly for his effort in the midst of crush to fashion a foreword for this book.

Thanks also to Beverley Bird for her ideas, her editing and for the occasional research field trip to the Napa Valley in the furtherance of this project.

And thanks to Lissa Asebo for her help in evaluating many of the restaurants considered for the book.

Errors or updates may be reported by emailing the author at "RichDraw@aol.com". Use the word "Correction" in the subject line.

13064004R00103

Made in the USA
San Bernardino, CA
07 July 2014